Hawaiian

Reef Animals

Hawaiian Reef Animals

REVISED EDITION

EDMUND HOBSON AND E. H. CHAVE

UNIVERSITY OF HAWAII PRESS

HONOLULU

Manufactured in Hong Kong

90 91 92 93 94 95 5 4 3 2 1

Library of Congress Cataloging-in-Publication Data

Hobson, Edmund S.

   Hawaiian reef animals / Edmund Hobson and E.H. Chave. — Rev. ed.

     p. cm.

   Includes bibliographical references.

   ISBN 0-8248-1307-3

   1. Fishes—Hawaii—Pictorial works.   2. Marine invertebrates-

-Hawaii—Pictorial works.   I. Chave, E. H.   II. Title.

QL636.5.H3H62   1990

597.092'59—dc20   89-20658

               CIP

Contents

Plates

Preface

There have been many additions to our knowledge of Hawaiian reef animals during the eighteen years since the first edition of this book was published. Many of the scientific names have changed as it was determined that species thought to occur only in Hawaii also live (with older names) elsewhere. This has been particularly true of the fishes, as shown especially by the energetic studies of John E. Randall of the Bernice P. Bishop Museum. The mollusks, one of the more complex groups of Hawaiian reef animals, were put in order by Dr. Alison Kay of the University of Hawaii, who culminated years of study with publication of her treatise on that group. Studies of marine turtles by George Balazs of the University of Hawaii and of the Hawaiian monk seal by a group under the direction of Dr. John Henderson of the National Marine Fisheries Service have provided much new information on these previously little-known animals. Margaret Titcomb of the Bernice P. Bishop Museum collaborated with Danielle Fellows, Mary Kawena Pukui, and Dennis Devaney to produce a storehouse of information in their report on native use of marine invertebrates. And the continued studies of reef-fish communities by one of the authors of this book, Edmund Hobson, have provided much new information and many new photographs for this revised edition.

The essence of the book, however, was established in the first edition, and the influence of those who contributed to that work remains very much in evidence. Of the individuals acknowledged above, Drs. Randall and Kay made especially meaningful contributions, and the earlier collaboration between Titcomb and Pukui describing native use of fishes was a rich source of information. Others making substantial contributions include David Hurd, Ruby Johnson, John Kuahiwinui, John Maciolek, Lloyd Richards, and Sidney Townsley.

Introduction

Hawaii, her land and the traditions of her people, has evolved intimately tied to the sea. The Islands themselves erupted from the ocean floor in times so recent that signs of their birth remain everywhere, and a marine tradition permeates all of man's history on these bits of land. Until very recent times, travel from one place to another, even on a single island, usually was over water, and most settlements were, and still are, along the shores. Sea life has traditionally been the major source of protein for Hawaiians, and probably every edible marine organism within their reach has been at one time or another a regular part of the diet. All forms of marine life —the fishes, corals, crustaceans, mollusks, even seaweeds—were grouped together by ancient Hawaiians as *i'a* (34).

All of the early Islanders were familiar with the reef's inhabitants, but it was with a select group of head fishermen, the *po'o lawai'a* (52), that fishing developed as a fine art. These respected men, numbering both commoners and royalty in their ranks, took great pride in their thorough command of the fishing trade. The profession carried with it a vast legacy of knowledge. Each generation of fishermen augmented this legacy with knowledge gained from their own experience before passing it on to their apprentices. The legacy included not only knowledge of techniques and equipment, but also of the habits of the different marine creatures—their specific habitats, food preferences, spawning, and migrations. For the *po'o lawai'a*, fishing was not a haphazard game of chance, but a science in which the technique used to catch a certain species was based on understanding the habits of that particular animal. As was custom, the spoken word and personalized instruction were the only means of transmitting this knowledge from one generation to the next. With the passing of the old ways, too many years passed before chroniclers of Hawaiian history, pen in hand, probed the fading memories of those few aged fishermen who remembered how it was. Consequently, there remains today only a fragmented picture of the fishing knowledge of the early Hawaiians.

There was of course no break in the use of fish as food. But as people from other cultures flooded into the Islands during the last half of the nineteenth century, the ways of fishing, like so many other Hawaiian customs, experienced rapid change. The Japanese, especially, possessing a rich and proud tradition as fishermen in their own right, introduced many new techniques and modified Hawaiian ones. For example, the throw net, which today approaches a cliché in its association with native Hawaiian fishermen, was actually introduced by the Japanese during the 1890s (7). Thus the fishing practices of Hawaii today are a rich blend of the more durable practices of early Islanders and of introduced techniques, many of which were modified to suit Island conditions.

Today the role of fishes in early Hawaiian beliefs and social custom is better known than is the ancient fishing knowledge. Although generally diluted or discredited by exposure to the outer world, the folklore persists. Even when credence has been lost, many of the old beliefs have lived on if only because their telling makes a good story. To many of today's Islanders, the old beliefs are no more than quaint relics of another time; but among others, especially those of Hawaiian blood, many of the ancient beliefs are still deeply respected.

The ancient Hawaiians acknowledged many gods, and their belief influenced even the most ordinary of everyday activities. The god of fishes and fishermen was Kū'ulakai, who was worshiped along with his wife Hinapukui'a and son 'Ai'ai (52). Small fishing shrines, called *ko'a* and usually dedicated to Kū'ulakai, were located near the water's edge. Many of these were sacred to certain fish. For example, on the 'Ewa side of Koko Head, on O'ahu, a shrine called Palialea was sacred to mullet (37). These were simple structures, frequently no more than a flat stone on a rocky point. In fact, so simple were these structures that the remaining ones easily go unnoticed by the uninitiated. An individual designated as the guardian of the *ko'a* offered here the first fish of each catch. Significantly, even though the *heiau*, temples of the old religion, have been deserted for over a century, some Hawaiians still place offerings at a *ko'a*, especially when fishing is poor.

Fishermen believed that Kū'ulakai controlled all fishes in the sea and that the whim of this god determined fishing success. Beyond this, each fisherman also venerated a personal god, or *'aumakua*. This deity inhabited the body of some individual plant or animal and looked over, and protected, its devotee; fishermen usually found their *'aumākua* in sea creatures. Certain individual sharks, in particular, were considered the physical embodiment of an *'aumakua*. Eels, porpoises, and *'opihi* were also among forms venerated by various fishermen (5). And whenever an abnormally colored or shaped fish was inadvertently taken, it was returned to the sea lest it prove to be an *'aumakua* (52). Individual creatures recognized as *'aumakua* were offered food and prayer daily at certain points along the shore; neglect of this duty invited disastrous consequences.

Certain fishes, considered among the most highly esteemed foods, were regarded as appropriate offerings to the gods; generally red or white fishes were used. Pigs were among the more important ceremonial offerings, but frequently could not be obtained when needed. As Hawaiians believed that living things on land had their counterparts in the sea, certain fishes were recognized as equivalent to the pig and were used in its place. Such fishes were known as *pua'a kai*, or sea pigs. Further, Hawaiians believed magic to be inherent in the meanings of words, and, as many Hawaiian words have multiple meanings, frequently a fish was chosen as an offering because its name carried a meaning pertinent to the situation (52).

The ancient Hawaiians recognized that fishes are a resource that must be actively conserved. The fishermen knew there was a limit to the numbers of fish they could take from a given spot before it was no longer productive. Sadly, this concept has had little impact on the fishing practices of latter-day Islanders, and many species that remained abundant during generations of intensive, but controlled, fishing by early Islanders have become rare during the past century.

A major instrument of conservation in ancient Hawaii was the *kapu*, or forbidden practices (52). Among the many *kapu* that regulated the consumption of fishes was one that forbade the taking of many species during certain times of the year, periods that often corresponded to the spawning seasons of the species. The penalty for violating the *kapu* was severe; frequently, instant death awaited the individual who consumed a forbidden fish. And even should the violator of a *kapu* escape detection by those enforcing the *kapu*, it was assumed that the action had been witnessed by the gods, and that surely they would deal with the violator in their own way. Not surprisingly, the fish and game laws of that time were far more closely adhered to than those of our day.

The old ways passed as newcomers from other lands and diverse cultures arrived to become Islanders themselves. The resulting hybrid culture was less attuned to the natural conditions of the Islands than had been the culture it supplanted. To this day, there have been earnest and continuing efforts to get back into step with nature, but success has been elusive. The accelerating complexity of present Hawaiian society has made the enormousness of this task staggering.

Today Hawaii is a marine science center. Internationally recognized authorities in a wide range of specialties, particularly those concerned with tropical seas, study in the Islands' various scientific establishments: the University of Hawaii, Bishop Museum, National Marine Fisheries Service Laboratory, Oceanic Institute, and the Fish and Game Division of the state's Department of Land and Natural Resources. Much of this study concerns marine life on Hawaiian reefs; indeed, not since the days of the *po'o lawai'a* has so much general knowledge of Hawaiian marine life been available.

In this book we strive to discuss those aspects of Hawaiian reef animals that have drawn the attention of Islanders past and present. We emphasize the role of these animals in early Hawaiian folklore and traditions, but also include topics that have excited the interest of more recent residents.

Plate 1. Gray reef shark, *Carcharhinus amblyrhynchos.*

The
Vertebrates

Animals
with backbones

Plate 2. Whitetipped reef shark, *Triaenodon obesus*.

Sharks

Among creatures of the sea, sharks have been especially meaningful to Hawaiian Islanders. In the Hawaiian language, sharks, in general, are called *manō*. More than any other marine animal, sharks were worshiped in ancient times as *'aumākua*. Generally, shark *'aumākua* were believed to have had human origins—many were traced to aborted human fetuses that had been cast into the sea (5). Perhaps owing to its appearance, the partly formed fetus may have suggested a supernatural union. The fetus was believed to return to its family as an *'aumakua*, spiritually embodied in the form of a shark. Thereafter, members of that family, including descendants, worshiped what they believed to be the individual shark that represented their *'aumakua*. To them, shark meat, as food, was *kapu*, and they were required to make regular offerings of food and prayer at the place along the shore where their shark *'aumakua* lived. In return, they believed, the shark would protect them from harm while at sea and also would bring them good fishing. Sharks were the *'aumākua* of families among both the royalty and commoners: the family of King Kalākaua worshiped a shark as their *'aumakua*. Although regarded as a god, an *'aumakua* nevertheless was also considered a servant of the family.

Sometimes all the inhabitants of a coastal region regarded a single shark as their *'aumakua*, and its name, history, appearance, place of abode, and other individual characteristics were well known to all. A member of a certain family charged with performing appropriate offerings to their *'aumakua* was known as a *kahu*. The position of *kahu* was hereditary and handed down within a family from one generation to the next (5). The people believed that the *kahu* was endowed with special powers because of his intimate relation with the *'aumakua* and therefore he exerted great influence over the community. Although the shark *'aumakua* was generally thought to protect its devotees, the *kahu* was frequently feared by the community (5). It was believed, for example, that a *kahu* could transmit disease to those who displeased him, and in a village struck by sickness the malady was often attributed to the local *kahu*. Taking advantage of the power he held in the minds of the people, a *kahu* sometimes terrorized his neighbors by adorning himself with trappings that made him resemble a shark and by speaking in a squeaky falsetto tone of voice (34).

It was believed that most shark *'aumākua* could take human form at will—hence sharks believed to be *'aumākua* were collectively called *manō kanaka*, or shark men. There are many old Hawaiian stories of shark men who, in their human form, looked like other men except in having the mouth of a shark on their backs, and who became sharks upon leaping into the sea. A typical story tells of Nenewe, a shark man, who lived beside a path to the sea in Waipi'o Valley, on the island of Hawai'i (10). Nenewe hailed swimmers and fishermen taking the path and inquired of their destination. Then, armed with this knowledge, he raced ahead on an alternate trail and, taking his shark form in the sea, devoured his victims when they arrived. Because of such folklore, many Hawaiians even today are reluctant to reveal an intent to go fishing.

The submarine homes of the shark deities were revered by the early Islanders, and even into modern times these locations have been considered by many to be sacred places. The twentieth century assumed a collision course with ancient Hawaiian beliefs when, in 1913, the U.S. Navy began building the large drydock in Pearl Harbor. The site chosen was known to belong to the shark goddess Ka'ahupāhau, but the Navy ignored the warnings of old Hawaiians. Construction proceeded without incident until the drydock was nearly completed. Then, in a sudden roar of splintering timbers, the entire structure collapsed. Why? The official record is not clear. Nevertheless, when work was begun again a priest of the old religion, a *kahuna*, was enlisted to appease Ka'ahupāhau. After appropriate prayers, and a ceremonious offering, work on the drydock was resumed. This time the job was successfully completed. Later, when the water was pumped from the drydock, the remains of a 14-foot shark were found at the bottom (45). Those unwilling to accept the influence of Ka'ahupāhau in this incident can readily cite coincidence—but there are still many who sincerely believe otherwise.

The most common sharks around Hawaiian reefs are the various gray sharks of the family Carcharhinidae. Many old Hawaiian names probably refer to these sharks, but whether these names correspond to species recognized today, or just to certain individuals, is uncertain. Examples include *manō pā'ele* (black-smudged *manō*), *manō lele wa'a* (canoe-jumping *manō*), and *(manō pahāha* (thick-necked *manō*) (52).

It has long been recognized that several varieties of gray sharks live in Hawaiian waters, but early ichthyologists assumed that most occur only around these islands. As a result of a shark-fishing program carried out by the late Dr. Albert L. Tester in the 1960s, however, enough specimens were put into the hands of specialists to determine that all the species of gray sharks in Hawaii are wide-ranging in tropical seas.

The gray shark most often encountered around Hawaiian reefs is the sandbar shark, *Carcharhinus milberti*. This species, which is also common in the tropical western Atlantic, rarely exceeds 6 feet in Hawaii. An underwater swimmer will find it to be a timid animal that scurries away upon meeting a human. Also common is the Galapagos shark, *C. galapagensis*, which was once thought to be limited to islands off western tropical America, but is now known to live around tropical oceanic islands worldwide. Although some Galapagos sharks grow to over 12 feet long, most that occur around reefs are much smaller. The shark that swims up to investigate a swimmer near the surface often turns out to be a Galapagos shark. Such encounters simply display its curious nature, however, and upon satisfying this curiosity the Galapagos shark usually fades off into the blue waters from which it appeared. A third species, the gray reef shark, *C. amblyrhynchos* (Plate 1), is the most abundant gray shark around most islands of the central Pacific, including those of the Hawaiian archipelago northwest of Ni'ihau. But except for some localized concentrations, such as occur around Molokini, an islet between Maui and Kaho'olawe, the species is infrequently encountered around the major Hawaiian Islands. The gray reef shark seldom exceeds about 7 feet in length, but is known to have attacked humans.

Another species, the whitetipped reef shark, *Triaenodon obesus* (Plate 2), is included here among the gray sharks even though many ichthyologists consider it more closely related to another group of sharks. The whitetipped reef shark is abundant on reefs throughout the tropical Pacific, including those of the northwestern part of the Hawaiian archipelago, but it is not abundant around the major Hawaiian Islands. Nevertheless, because the species frequents shallow water and tends to remain in localized areas, it is seen regularly near the relatively few major-island reefs that it inhabits. For example, it is a familiar sight around the reefs off Ke'ei and Hōnaunau in Kona. Unlike the gray sharks considered above, which must swim constantly to keep oxygen-supplying water flowing over their gills, the whitetipped reef shark can pump water over its gills while at rest on the sea floor. A diver peering into a cave may be startled to discover one or more of these sharks resting in the shadows.

Two species of hammerheads occur in Hawaiian waters, the scalloped hammerhead, *Sphyrna lewini*, and the smooth hammerhead, *Sphyrna zygaena*. Both grow to over 12 feet long, but only the former is abundant. So far as is known, the early Hawaiians recognized only one hammerhead, referring to it as *manō kihikihi*. Although usually they frequent deep water offshore, female scalloped hammerheads come into shallow, sheltered waters during the summer to bear their young. At that time they are especially numerous in Kāne'ohe Bay, on O'ahu. Otherwise, hammerheads are not ordinarily seen near the reefs.

Early Hawaiian stories often tell of *niuhi*, a species of man-eating shark that was much feared by the Islanders. There are references to the eyes of this shark being luminous at night, as in the old chant:

Niuhi with fiery eyes
That flamed in the deep blue sea.
Alas! and alas!
When flowers the wili-wili tree
That is the time when the shark-god bites.
Alas! I am seized by the huge shark!
O blue sea, O dark sea,
Foam-mottled sea of Kane!
What pleasure I took in my dancing!
Alas, now consumed by the monster shark. (11)

Fishing for *niuhi* was a great event in ancient times—the sport of royalty. In anticipation, a great store of bait was accumulated. Human flesh was a favorite bait with many chiefs, not only because it was easier to obtain than pig, but its use also provided the chiefs an opportunity to eliminate persons who had fallen from favor. Kamehameha I, a renowned shark hunter, kept his victims imprisoned near the great Moʻokini *heiau*, near Hāwī on the island of Hawaiʻi. After the victims had been cut up, their flesh was allowed to decompose for several days, thus enhancing its effectiveness as shark bait (7).

One report describes details of an expedition to capture a *niuhi* (4). A fleet of canoes, laden with bait, and with the *poʻo lawaiʻa* and a *kahuna* in the lead, sailed to waters known to be frequented by this great shark. Once at anchor on the fishing ground, they cast great quantities of bait into the sea, for only after the waters for miles around carried the scent—a process that usually took several days—could the *niuhi* be expected to appear. When it arrived, the monster was fed huge quantities of food, which had been mixed liberally with pounded *ʻawa*, a narcotic herb of the pepper family. Gradually the *niuhi* became lethargic to the point that a noose could be slipped around its head. This was the climax. Once this had been accomplished, the fleet raised anchor and headed home. Groggy with *ʻawa*, satiated with food, and tethered with a line, the now docile *niuhi* followed the canoes, periodically receiving *ʻawa*-laced food to ensure its continued cooperation. At home, the fishermen led the stupefied shark into shallow water, where it was stranded and finally killed. Its flesh was not eaten, but the teeth of the shark were prized as weapons, and portions of its skeleton and skin were coveted by the fishermen, who believed that the possession of these objects would endow them with courage. And he who had actually placed the noose around the head of the *niuhi* was confident of being forever victorious in battle.

In the literature of recent times it has been assumed that *niuhi* was the white shark, *Carcharodon carcharias*, and indeed it may well have been. But a good case can be made that it was instead the tiger shark, *Galeocerdo cuvieri*. White sharks are seen only rarely in Hawaiian waters today; unless they were more numerous in ancient times, it does not seem that they could have accounted for the attention generated by *niuhi*. Tiger sharks, on the other hand, are regular inhabitants of Island waters, and individuals over 14 feet long weighing a ton or more are not uncommon. Such a monster could not have failed to deeply impress early Islanders, and yet no Hawaiian name has been linked with the tiger shark, even though this distinctive animal has many specific morphological characteristics that set it apart from other sharks. Certainly the tiger shark is world renowned as a man-eater; indeed, of the sharks that regularly frequent Hawaiian waters, the tiger shark represents the greatest threat to humans.

Despite the strong shark tradition of the Islands, Hawaiian waters are among the safest in tropical seas. In the more than 100 years since records were first kept, only seventeen people have been injured by sharks—five fatally. This is remarkably few, considering the countless numbers of people who regularly have entered Island waters for work and play over the years.

During most of this time there was a viable shark fishery in Hawaii, with the catch being marketed largely as an ingredient of fish cakes. However, the fishery suffered a mortal blow in the early 1940s, when legislation was passed requiring that the ingredients of fish cakes be listed on the package, and consumers rejected the use of shark meat. The resulting demise of the fishery was both unnecessary and unfortunate: unnecessary because shark meat is in fact highly palatable fare when properly prepared, and unfortunate because with little doubt the fishery kept the numbers of sharks in Hawaiian coastal waters at a low level. Shark populations are especially vulnerable to fishing, compared to those of most other fishes. This is largely because the developing young are carried by the females for a long period, and because only a relatively few young are produced by each female during the breeding season. In the years following the end of the shark fishery, sightings of these animals increased, and it was the opinion of many experts that the numbers of sharks in Hawaiian coastal waters was on the upswing. Then in 1958 a tiger shark attacked and fatally injured a fifteen-year-old surfer on Windward Oʻahu. Public alarm crystallized with this incident, and support was generated leading to the several shark-fishing programs supervised by Dr. Tester over the next decade. In addition to much-needed information on shark biology, these efforts demonstrated that even a limited fishing effort, when systematically conducted, can effectively reduce the numbers of sharks that are active in nearshore waters.

Eels

Most eels in Hawaii are morays, of the family Muraenidae. Collectively called *puhi* by Islanders, these predators are denizens of cracks and crevices in the reef. Because they venture only infrequently into the open, their great abundance cannot be appreciated by the casual observer. Generally only those few that protrude their heads from reef crevices are seen by day, even though the morays include more species than any other family of Hawaiian reef fishes except the wrasse family, Labridae. It was long assumed that morays are nocturnal and emerge from the reef to feed at night. Although this is true of at least one Hawaiian species, *Gymnothorax petelli* (Plate 3), most remain hidden at all hours. Indeed, morays are adapted to activity within reef crevices, and at least most should capture prey best there (22). Many are quick to detect injured fishes, however, and frequently are lured from their hiding places after the spear of a diver has found its mark.

Moray eels were the *'aumākua* of many early Hawaiians (52). One well-known eel-god, called Ko'ona, was worshiped by the people of Wailau on the windward coast of Moloka'i. Many heroic deeds are attributed to this deity, and to this day a large cave on the rock shore is said to have been formed when Ko'ona caused the cliffside to fall on a large shark that had invaded the area. According to legend (35), Ko'ona met his end after raiding the fishponds of Kū'ulakai, god of fishermen, at Hāna, Maui. It was 'Ai'ai, son of Kū'ulakai, who led several canoes on the expedition that destroyed Ko'ona. A large hook was secured to a long line and baited. Weighting himself with stones, 'Ai'ai dived with the hook to the opening of a submarine cave known to harbor Ko'ona. When the huge *puhi* took the bait and was hooked, the canoes trailed the line to shore at Lehaula. Here it was taken up by the people of the area, who pulled together and hauled the giant *puhi* onto the beach. Three *'a'ā* stones, hurled by 'Ai'ai at the stranded eel-god, provided the death blows. On the beach at this place today a rock formation 30 feet long is said to be the remains of Ko'ona's backbone, and another group of rocks awash in the sea a short distance away is claimed to have been the creature's jaw bones.

Despite the probably exaggerated reports by divers of giants over 10 feet long, *puhi* on Hawaiian reefs today do not appear to exceed a length of more than about 5 or 6 feet. The larger eels are a small minority; most Hawaiian species are not longer than about 2 feet when fully grown (14). An example is *Gymnothorax meleagris* (Plate 4),

Plate 3. Moray eel, *Gymnothorax petelli*, on the reef at night.

Plate 4. Moray eel, *Gymnothorax meleagris* (puhi ʻōniʻo).

known to early Hawaiians as *puhi ʻōniʻo* (spotted *puhi*); this *puhi* characteristically protrudes its head from the coral and is perhaps the moray seen most often by snorkelers swimming over the reef.

There are many Hawaiian names for the different *puhi*, but, as is true of the gray sharks, these names are often difficult to match with species recognized today. Such names were applied only to the larger members of a species; finger-size individuals of all species were referred to collectively as *puhi ʻōilo* (young *puhi*), and those up to about 2 feet as *puhi ʻauʻaukī* (*ti* stem) (52).

The *puhi* were heavily fished by early Hawaiians. Very small individuals were frequently caught by hand, a technique known as *ʻini ʻiniki puhi* (52). In this method, the fisherman placed a small octopus, *heʻe pali*, in the palm of his left hand, allowing the tentacles to dangle between his fingers in rocky shallows where small *puhi* were known to abound. When an eel emerged to seize one of the tentacles, the fisherman used his right hand to pull the octopus slowly from his palm and toward his wrist, an action that withdrew the tentacles from between his fingers. The small eel followed, and when the fisherman saw the eel's head appear between his fingers he snapped his fist closed, securing the tiny creature in his grasp. Often several eels were captured simultaneously in this way, but understandably the method was not used to catch larger morays. In fact, when a big *puhi* appeared fishermen often would leave the area.

The larger eels were fished, but the fishermen used care to avoid injury. Hook and line, or a spear, were used. In wading depths, larger *puhi* often were chased into scoop nets, whereupon the fisherman raced across the shallows, trying to reach shore before his writhing captive could struggle free (7). Once landed, *puhi* were dispatched with two blows of a mallet—one blow to the head, the other to the tail (30). Because an eel frequently is stunned more effectively by a blow to the tail than to the head, many Island fishermen even now contend that an eel's brain is in its tail. This anomaly can be traced to the fact that the moray's brain is encased in an especially heavy and strong skull, an adaptation to the animal's habit of wedging its way among the narrow openings within the reef.

The larger eels were feared by Islanders, and justifiably so, because these animals can inflict serious injury. The most feared, *Gymnothorax flavimarginatus* (Plate 5), was called *puhi paka* (fierce *puhi*). This heavy-bodied species is the most frequently seen of the larger *puhi* and was often sought by the more adventuresome fishermen. There are other large eels, with more vicious dispositions, that are better equipped to inflict injury, the dark brown species *Enchelynassa canina*, for example. Nevertheless, *puhi paka* probably represent the greatest poten-

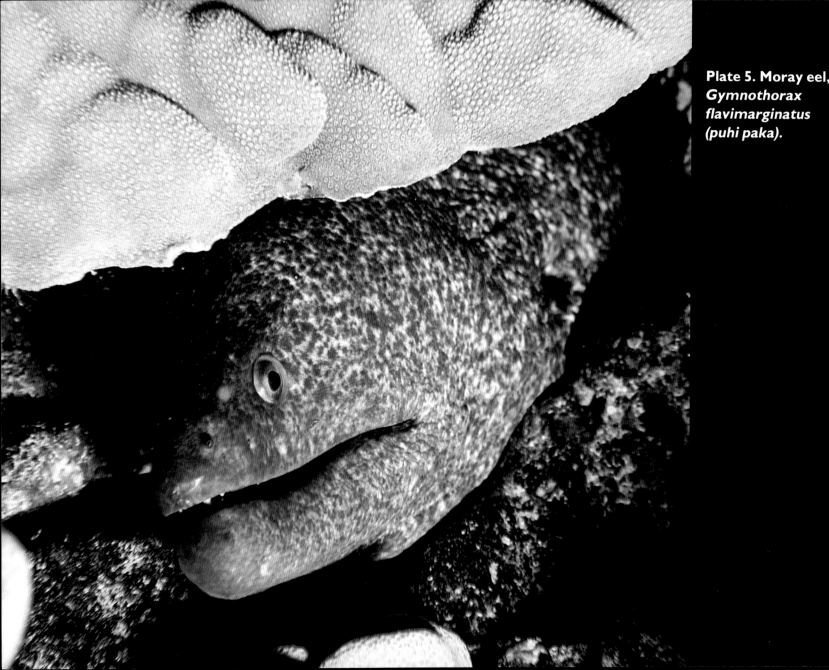

Plate 5. Moray eel, *Gymnothorax flavimarginatus (puhi paka).*

Plate 6. White eel, *Conger cinereus (puhi ūhā)*, at night.

tial danger because they are so numerous. A writer on Lāna'i had this to say of the *puhi paka* one hundred years ago: "He often baffles the efforts of the fishermen. He will swallow the hook and bite the line in two. He will force himself out of a net, and if you have got him with a stout hook and line you must tear him to pieces before you can drag him out of the hole in the rocks in which he has set and braced himself. . . . He will take off a toe, or snap off an exposed naked foot, if he gets a chance. . . . He devours everything" (52).

This report describes accurately the difficulties of catching *puhi paka*, but exaggerates its destructive potential. Because the needlelike teeth of most morays are adapted for grasping prey, not cutting, it is unlikely that even the largest moray could "snap off" a human foot. Usually the moray that strikes a human hand or foot does so in error. Most such instances occur when an unseen *puhi* strikes the hand of a diver who has reached back into a crevice for a lobster or an attractive shell. The moray in this situation probably feels threatened or mistakes the hand for prey. Generally, it will release its hold as soon as the error is recognized, and divers that can resist the natural impulse to pull free may well escape with no more than a series of puncture wounds. Unfortunately, such presence of mind in this situation is rare, and a hand is often severely slashed when forcibly wrenched from between the backward-projecting teeth of the moray.

The larger morays are primarily fish-eaters, and their fanglike teeth are adapted for grasping mobile prey. Although most members of the family have this type of dentition, morays in the genus *Echidna*, of which three species are known to occur in Hawaii, possess instead blunt pebblelike teeth that are adapted for crushing. The prey of these blunt-snouted *puhi*, which grow to about 3 feet long, are mostly large, heavily shelled crustaceans.

Not all the prominent eels on the reef are morays. One of the best-known Hawaiian species is the white eel, *Conger cinereus* (Plate 6), of the family Congridae. This fish, called *puhi ūhā* by Islanders, grows to about 4 feet long, but is not a threat to humans. It remains hidden in caves during the day, but searches for prey in the open at night. The *puhi ūhā* has always been a favorite food of Hawaiians; one early writer described the white eel as ". . . a fish of which chiefs were fond . . . considered choicer than wives . . ." (52).

Lizardfishes

The lizardfishes, collectively called *'ulae* by Hawaiians, are well named. Their appearance is reptilian, both in body form and also in the way they rest motionless, but

Plate 7. Lizardfish, _Synodus variegatus_ ('ulae).

alert, on the sea floor. They constitute the family Syn-odontidae, of which three are often observed around Hawaiian reefs: *Synodus variegatus* (Plate 7), *S. binota-tus*, and *Saurida flamma* (40). Usually these predators sit on a patch of sand among the corals, where their cryptic coloration makes them difficult to see. In this pose, fully exposed, yet effectively concealed, they wait for small fishes to come within striking range. Sometimes they bury themselves—all except their eyes and the tips of their snouts—in the sand. From this position, attacking with an explosive rush upward, they seize even the most wary prey between fang-rimmed jaws.

Anglerfishes

The anglerfishes, family Antennariidae, are unusual crea-tures. Those that live on the reef look more like a lump on the sea floor than a fish (Plate 8), an illusion height-ened by their characteristic lack of movement. Nine spe-cies have been reported from Hawaiian reefs, but only a few are seen with any regularity, and none are abundant (40). They rarely swim above the substrate, and when one moves it usually does so with what looks like an awk-ward crawl, its jointed pectoral fins being used much like arms. But the most unusual feature of many anglerfishes is the modified first spine of their dorsal fins. This spine,

which is far forward on the head, has transformed into a flexible "fishing pole," complete with a fleshy "lure," or bait, at the end. Waving this bait in front of its mouth, the anglerfish waits until a small fish is attracted. Once the little fish has approached within range, the anglerfish springs open its mouth and sucks in the prey.

Soldierfishes and Squirrelfishes

Soldierfishes and squirrelfishes, of the family Holocentri-dae, are prominent on Hawaiian reefs. The former are known by the Hawaiian name 'ū'ū, or probably more often today by the Japanese equivalent *menpachi*, where-as the latter are known by the Hawaiian name 'ala'ihi. The coloration of all is predominantly red, and although some occasionally exceed a length of 12 inches, most are considerably smaller than this.

Including three very similar species that generally are not distinguished by Islanders, the soldierfishes, or *men-pachi*, are numerous on shallow reefs. Science classifies these as *Myripristis amaena* (Plate 9), *M. berndti*, and *M. kuntee*. They are among the fishes most frequently hunt-ed by spear fishermen and, being prized as food, bring a high price in Hawaiian markets today. *Menpachi* are noc-turnal, a fact consistent with their very large eyes. They assemble in submarine caves during the day, but at night

Plate 8. Anglerfish, *Antennarius coccineus*.

Plate 9. Soldierfish, *Myripristis amaena* (menpachi, or 'ū'ū), in a cave during the day.

**Plate 10. Squirrelfish,
Neoniphon sammara
('ala 'ihi).**

Plate 11. Squirrelfish, *Sargocentron xantherythrum* ('ala 'ihi), under a ledge during the day.

venture out and hunt small prey in the darkened waters over the reef (22).

The squirrelfishes, or *'ala'ihi*, are classified today in the genera *Neoniphon* and *Sargocentron*. Several forms were distinguished by early Islanders, including *'ala'ihi piliko'a* (*'ala'ihi* clinging to coral), *'ala'ihi kala loa* (*'ala'ihi* with long spike), and *'ala'ihi lā kea* (*'ala'ihi* with white dorsal fin). It is uncertain, however, how these specific names relate to the six species of *'ala'ihi* recognized today as common on shallow reefs: *Neoniphon sammara* (Plate 10), *Sargocentron diadema*, *S. punctatissimum*, *S. spiniferum*, *S. tiere*, and *S. xantherythrum* (Plate 11). In contrast to the highly palatable *menpachi*, the various *'ala'ihi* are not used much as food today (14); nevertheless, it is said that *'ala'ihi* were the favorite fish of King Kamehameha III (52). Similar to *menpachi*, *'ala'ihi* are nocturnal animals that shelter themselves in reef crevices by day and forage in the open under cover of darkness. But whereas the *menpachi* feed in the waters above the reef, the *'ala'ihi* find their prey close to the reef (22).

Trumpetfish and Cornetfish

The trumpetfishes, family Aulostomidae, are represented in Hawaii by one species—*Aulostomus chinensis* (Plate 12), called *nūnū* by Hawaiians. The very similar cornetfishes, family Fistulariidae, are also represented in the Islands by just one species—*Fistularia commersoni*. Both of these elongate fishes, with their long flute-shaped snouts, are distributed widely through warm waters of the Indian and Pacific oceans. The anatomies of the two are similar: perhaps the most recognizable difference lies in the long filament that streams from the center of the cornetfish's tail, a feature the trumpetfish lacks. The colors of each are more distinguishing: three color varieties occur among trumpetfish—plain brown, brown with lighter markings, and plain yellow; in contrast, the cornetfish is always pale green with lighter markings. There is also a difference in size: whereas the trumpetfish does not exceed a length of about 2 feet, the cornetfish often grows to 5 feet long, and more (14).

Both species are predators. The trumpetfish regularly captures both crustaceans and fishes, but the larger cornetfish is almost exclusively a fish-eater (22). On casual glance, the long tubular snouts of these fishes suggest diets of very small prey, but in fact the snouts are capable of much expansion, and surprisingly large prey are captured. The expansion is so sudden that a strong vacuum is created within that literally sucks prey into their mouths. In fact, the mechanism so effectively snares large prey that it occasionally leads to disaster when one of these

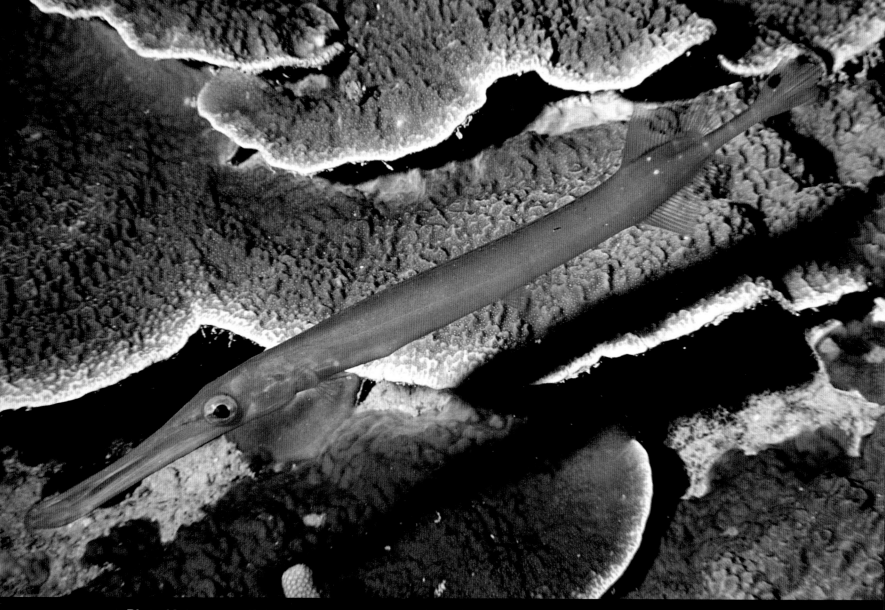

Plate 12. Trumpetfish, *Aulostomus chinensis* (nūnū).

predators chokes to death on an oversized organism that has become tightly wedged in its throat.

Their feeding mechanism is effective only at short range, however, and because neither species is a strong swimmer they must rely on stealth to get close to their quarry. Sometimes they approach prey from behind the body of a large animal that grazes on seaweeds, such as a parrotfish. This tactic is especially effective because many smaller fishes, like wrasses, characteristically assemble where herbivores are grazing. The smaller fishes congregate there and capture organisms uncovered when the seaweeds are cropped from the ocean floor. But the attraction can be fatal, as these smaller fishes sometimes fall prey to a trumpetfish or cornetfish lurking in the shadow of the big herbivore. Nevertheless, despite the frequency of such attacks, they capture most of their prey by quietly gliding along in the shadows of the reef, striking creatures that have carelessly strayed too far from cover (9).

Scorpionfishes

The scorpionfishes, family Scorpaenidae, owe their name to the venomous stings that they can inflict with their fin spines. These spines are grooved, and within the grooves are venom glands (15). Although there are 17 species of scorpionfishes on the nearshore reefs (40), all but one generally go unnoticed because they are highly cryptic and move only infreqently.

The one member of this family readily seen on Hawaiian reefs, the lionfish, *Pterois sphex* (Plate 13), represents the greatest threat to humans. This is among the most ornate of reef fishes, and highly sought after by aquarists. Because generally it rests motionless on the reef and seemingly is fearless, the capture of this fish might seem a simple matter. But its venom is particularly virulent, and even experienced collectors usually are stung at least once before learning to exercise special care. Individuals of this species reportedly grow to about 10 inches long (14), but those seen on the reef usually are less than half this size. It is a nocturnal predator that feeds mainly on crustaceans, particularly shrimps, and generally occurs in exposed positions only at night (22).

The largest of the scorpionfishes common on Hawaiian reefs is *Scorpaenopsis cacopsis* (Plate 14), known to Islanders as *nohu 'omakaha*. Although it grows to a length of at least 20 inches (14), and typically rests in exposed positions, this fish usually goes unnoticed. In contrast to the lionfish, which is conspicuous in its surroundings, the *nohu 'omakaha* looks much like a part of the reef. Going unseen, this predator snaps open its cavernous mouth and sucks in small fishes and octopuses

Plate 13. Lionfish,
Pterois sphex.

Plate 14. Scorpionfish,
Scorpaenopsis cacopsis
(nohu).

that come near (22). This tactic may be aided by a small white appendage carried just inside the lower lip. Often this appendage is moving and highly visible while *nohu 'omakaha* is otherwise motionless and virtually unseen, and it may function to lure prey within range of capture (23).

Sea Basses and Groupers

Sea basses and groupers, family Serranidae, are prominent fishes on most tropical reefs, but for reasons not fully understood neither is a major presence in Hawaii. Most Hawaiian sea basses are members of the subfamily Anthiinae, which are small, colorful fishes that feed on zooplankton and generally inhabit the deeper reefs. One of these, *Anthias ventralis* (Plate 15), is frequently seen by scuba divers at depths below 80 feet. Of the groupers, *Epinephelus quernus* (Plate 16), known to early Islanders as *hāpu'u*, is numerous on shallow reefs at the northwestern end of the archipelago, but occurs only in deeper water around the major islands. The member of this family most often encountered on shallow reefs, however, is not native to Hawaiian waters. This is the grouper *Cephalopholis argus*, a dark fish with bright blue spots that was introduced to Hawaii from the Society Islands by the Department of Land and Natural Resources in the 1950s.

Flagtail

The Hawaiian flagtail, called *āholehole* by Islanders, is *Kuhlia sandvicensis*, of the family Kuhliidae (Plate 17). This silvery fish with large eyes grows to a length of about 12 inches and is unusual in living in fresh water as well as in the sea (14). During the day the adults school in the shallows or, more frequently, secrete themselves in caves. They leave these places at nightfall, however, and during the night forage above the reef on tiny crustaceans (22).

The *āholehole* was a favorite of early Hawaiians, both as food and as a ceremonial sacrifice. Many chiefs valued its delicate flavor. Royalty at Hilo were known to have *āholehole*, still living, brought to them from the fishing grounds at Puna, over 20 miles away. To keep the fish alive during the long trip overland, they were wrapped in seaweed (52). Ceremonial roles of the *āholehole* were several. It was regarded as a "sea pig" *(pua'a kai)* and as such could be substituted in ceremonies calling for a pig when that animal was not available. It was also offered in ceremonies requiring a white fish. *Hole*, a component of the word, means "to strip away," and so this fish was sacrificed when the object was to dispel evil spirits (52). In the early days of immigration to Hawaii, Caucasians sometimes were called *āholehole* because of their white skin (52).

Plate 15. Longfin sea bass, *Anthias ventralis*.

Plate 16. Grouper, *Epinephelus quernus* *(hāpuʻu).*

Plate 17. Flagtail, *Kuhlia sandvicensis (āholehole).*

Bigeyes

Of the bigeyes, family Priacanthidae, two species occur on the nearshore reefs (40). The most frequently seen is *Heteropriacanthus cruentatus*, known to Hawaiians as *'āweoweo* (Plate 18). Growing to about 12 inches long and since early times a favorite of Hawaiian fishermen, the *'āweoweo* is widespread on reefs throughout the world's tropical seas. It can rapidly change color between reddish and silvery or assume a blotched pattern that is the two in combination. Like the *menpachi*, *'ala 'ihi*, and *āholehole*, the *'āweoweo* remains in the reef's shadows by day and hunts prey in exposed locations only at night (22).

Occasionally, great schools of *'āweoweo* appear near shore at night. Early Hawaiians witnessed this spectacular event with mixed emotions. Although pleased with this sudden abundance of an esteemed food fish, the people regarded the coming of these immense schools with sadness and awe, portending as they did the imminent death of a high chief (52).

Cardinalfishes

Although there are nine species of cardinalfishes on Hawaiian reefs (40), only two are seen frequently by the casual observer: *Apogon kallopterus* (Plate 19) and *A. taeniopterus*. The two are similar, and both were called *'upāpalu* by Hawaiians. They are the largest of the Hawaiian cardinalfishes, growing to about 9 inches long (14), and like other cardinalfishes are secretive by day. Individuals of *A. kallopterus*, however, frequently hover at the openings of their shadowy retreats during the day and are frequently seen there by divers. Like so many fishes that frequent reef caves by day, cardinalfishes emerge to feed at night, mostly on crustaceans (22). *'Upāpalu* are readily caught by fishermen after dark, especially under moonlight, and as a result many Islanders call them "moonlight Annies."

Jacks

The jacks, family Carangidae, are among the favorite catch of many Islanders that cast lines from rocky shores or use spears underwater. Among the largest and most sought after are species of the genera *Caranx*, *Pseudocaranx*, *Carangoides*, and *Gnathanodon*. To Islanders these are the various kinds of *ulua*. The young of most are collectively called *pāpio*, but generally the adults are distinguished from one another. Perhaps most often seen by divers is the blue *ulua*, *Caranx melampygus*, also known to Hawaiians as *'ōmilu* (Plate 20). Encountered less often

Plate 18. Bigeye, *Heteropriacanthus cruentatus* ('āweoweo)

Plate 19. Cardinalfish, *Apogon kallopterus* ('upāpalu).

Plate 20. Blue *ulua*, *Caranx melampygus* ('ōmilu).

above nearshore reefs around the major islands, but nevertheless a favored catch of shore fishermen there, is the white *ulua*, *Caranx ignobilis*, also called *ulua aukea* or *pā'ū'ū* (Plate 21). This species is important to commercial fishermen around the northwestern Hawaiian Islands, as is the pig *ulua*, *Pseudocaranx cheilio*, also known as *butaguchi* (Plate 22).

Several other species of *ulua* are similar in form and habits to the above, but the yellow *ulua*, *Gnathanodon speciosus*, also called *ulua pa'opa'o*, has habits that set it apart from other members of its family. Whereas the others use their abilities as strong swimmers to run down their prey in open water, the yellow *ulua*, which may attain a length of 3 feet, looks much like a grazing herbivore as it feeds head down with mouth thrust amid vegetation that carpets the sea floor in some places. Despite appearances, however, this fish is strictly a predator that works its highly protrusible, toothless jaws through the seaweeds to capture tiny animals hidden there (20).

When young, yellow *ulua* have habits very different from those of adults. Individuals just a fraction of an inch long occur close among the venomous tentacles of jellyfishes, a habit that offers them protection from predators. When they become too large for this, but still are less than an inch long, they become "pilots," swimming close before the snouts of much larger fishes, usually predators.

Because the eyes of most predators are on the sides of their heads, they cannot see the area immediately in front of their snouts. It is here that the tiny jacks swim—within inches of the predator's jaws, but out of sight and so probably unnoticed. Not only are the young jacks relatively safe from other predators when they swim immediately in front of their large companions, but also they are literally pushed along in the big animal's bow wave. By swimming with progressively larger fishes, these jacks can retain the piloting habit until they reach 5 or 6 inches long (19). Sometimes, mistaking a diver for a large fish, tiny yellow jacks assume a station immediately in front of the diver's face mask.

Snappers

Species of the snapper family Lutjanidae are dominant forms on most tropical reefs worldwide, but not in Hawaii. Presumably for reasons similar to those limiting groupers and sea basses, as discussed above, snappers did not become established on shallow Hawaiian reefs. The only native snapper commonly seen near Hawaiian shores is *Aphereus furcatus*, called *gurutsu*, which usually occurs as solitary individuals 8 to 12 inches long patrolling above the reef. This is not a typical coral-reef snapper, however. Nor is *Aprion virescens*, known as

Plate 21. White *ulua*, *Caranx ignobilis* (pā'ū'ū).

Plate 22. Pig ulua, *Pseudocaranx cheilio* (butaguchi).

Plate 23. Snapper, *Lutjanus fulvus (to'au).*

uku, a species of deeper water that grows up to 2 feet long, but is only occasionally seen near shore. Like *gurutsu*, *uku* near shore usually are solitary and swim above the reef.

Because coral-reef snappers are highly valued by sport fishermen and commercial fishermen alike, the Hawaii Department of Land and Natural Resources introduced from the Society Islands during the mid-1950s three species of coral-reef snappers. Two of these have since become well established on Hawaiian reefs: *Lutjanus fulvus* (Plate 23) and *Lutjanus kasmira*, both of which have retained their respective Tahitian names, *to'au* and *ta'ape*.

Goatfishes

The goatfishes, family Mullidae, are prominent members of the reef community and have been important to Islanders since early times. Most of them grow to about 16 inches long, and each has two large barbels under its chin —a characteristic they alone possess among Hawaiian nearshore fishes. With these barbels, the goatfishes probe sand and vegetation for small crustaceans, mollusks, and fishes that are hidden there (22).

Several different goatfishes are known by Hawaiians as *weke*. Probably the most numerous are *Mulloides vanicolensis*, known as *weke 'ula* (red *weke*; Plate 24), and *Mul-loides flavolineata*, known as *weke 'a'ā* (staring *weke*; Plate 25). Usually members of these species occur in schools that hover close to the sea floor or as individuals and in groups of two or three that forage in patches of sand on the reef.

Some *weke*, including *weke 'ula*, are reddish, whereas others, including *weke 'a'ā*, are whitish, so often they were used as sacrifices in ceremonies that called for red or white fish. The meaning of the word *weke*, "to open," also brought these animals into ceremonial use when a *kahuna* wanted to "open up" the mind of a subject and release evil thoughts (52).

Certain *weke* occasionally produce hallucinations, or morbid nightmares, in people who have eaten them. *Weke 'a'ā* have been implicated, but the major culprit has been *Upeneus taeniopterus*, which Islanders called *weke pahulu* (nightmare *weke*). Many claim the affliction occurs only after eating the brains of these fishes, but the symptoms have also appeared in people who have consumed only flesh of the bodies (16).

The nightmare-inducing qualities of certain *weke* were well known to early Islanders. Legend places the origin of the affliction on the island of Lāna'i, where it is related to the death of Pahulu, chief of evil spirits. As one story goes, Pahulu leaned over a pool of water and was struck by a stone hurled down on him by an adversary concealed

Plate 24. Goatfish, *Mulloides vanicolensis (weke 'ula)*. Two individuals at bottom center are hovering at a cleaning station.

Plate 25. Goatfish, *Mulloides flavolineata (weke 'a'ā)*, probing in sand for prey.

in a tree above. Pahulu fell lifeless into the water, but his spirit survived, embodied in the *weke pahulu*. It is because of this, according to the legend, that people who eat this fish are troubled with nightmares (52). Apparently in early times the effects were greatest on Lānaʻi, and the closer to this island the fish was caught the worse the nightmares (39). The pattern seems to have changed, however, as more recently the affliction has been limited to the islands of Kauaʻi and Molokaʻi, and then only during the months of June, July, and August (16).

Goatfishes common on Hawaiian reefs also include several species of the genus *Parupeneus*. The *kūmū*, *P. porphyreus*, has long been a great favorite of Islanders. This red fish was important in early times, both as food and as a ceremonial offering. It was one of the "sea pigs," as discussed above, and also was used when a *kahuna* demanded a red fish for ceremonial sacrifice. Other prominent species of *Parupeneus* are *P. pleurostigma*, called *malu*; *P. bifasciatus*, called *munu*; and *P. multifasciatus*, called *moano*. The *moano*, especially, has long been highly esteemed, as indicated by the old chant ". . . *A he moano kai lena, Ono! Ono!*," which means "The *moano* of the yellowish sea, delicious! delicious!" (52).

Still another species of *Parupeneus*, *P. cyclostomus*, is the largest of Hawaiian goatfishes, attaining lengths of about 2 feet (14). Today this species is known as *moano kea*, but probably it is also the fish early Hawaiians called *moano ukali ulua*. The translation of this name, "*moano* with *ulua* following," describes a common relation between this goatfish and the blue ulua, *Caranx melampygus*. The *moano kea* is the most piscivorous of the goatfishes, with exceptionally long barbels that it uses to reach into crevices and drive small fishes hidden there into the open. Frequently one or sometimes two or three blue *ulua* take advantage of this by following close behind and sharing with the goatfish prey thus made available (22).

Sea Chubs

The two species of sea chubs common above Hawaiian reefs—*Kyphosus vaigiensis* (Plate 26) and *K. bigibbus*—are very similar, and both are known to Islanders as *nenue*. They grow to about 2 feet long and feed mainly on drifting fragments of seaweeds (22). From a distance underwater most *nenue* appear plain gray, but some are seen to carry irregular yellow blotches, and a few are yellow all over. Occasionally white ones appear. Early Hawaiians believed that these aberrantly hued individuals protected the other *nenue* and referred to them as the *makua* (52).

Nenue are not regarded as food by most people today, at least partly because their strong odor is repugnant to

Plate 26. Sea chub, *Kyphosus vaigiensis (nenue)*.

modern tastes. In the old days, however, this same characteristic made them especially desirable. *Nenue* were in such high demand in ancient Hawaii that chiefs often reserved them for their own consumption (52). One can scarcely find a better example of the extent to which tastes have changed. A favored relish was prepared by chopping up into small pieces the head of a *nenue*, adding this to the fish's entrails, which have an especially penetrating odor of their own, and then seasoning the mixture with *kukui* nuts and chili pepper (52).

Butterflyfishes

The butterflyfishes, family Chaetodontidae, probably are more characteristic of coral reefs than is any other major family of fishes. Nevertheless, if Hawaiians distinguished most of the many butterflyfishes that inhabited their reefs, little evidence of this remains today. Perhaps they felt there was no need to distinguish one from another, because these relatively small bony fishes were little valued as food. Most seem to have been called, collectively, *lau hau* (*hau* leaf), or *kīkākapu* (*kīkā*, strong; *kapu*, taboo). This second name suggests that butterflyfishes had religious significance, as do references to them in various old chants, such as: "*He kākau kī'oki 'ōni'o i ka lae, he kī'oki 'o ke kīkākapu, 'o ka i'a kapu,*" which means,

"Marked with bars and streaks on the forehead, the *kīkākapu* is a sacred fish" (39).

Butterflyfishes are characterized by brilliant colors arranged in bold patterns; indeed, probably this is their single most outstanding feature. Although some elements of these color patterns conceal certain body features, for example the dark bars that conceal the eyes of many species (Plate 27), the overall effect is one of display. Possibly the display tells predators that this is a risky and unrewarding meal. There is little meat on these deep-bodied fishes, and with many having strong fin spines it would not seem worthwhile for a predator to chance getting one lodged in its throat (13).

It is likely, however, that the major benefit these fishes get from their distinctive colorations is increased ability to recognize others of their own kind. Probably butterflyfishes have a particular need for this because they often occur as many closely related species living together on one reef, with no one species especially numerous. For example, eleven species of the genus *Chaetodon* regularly coexist on Hawaiian reefs, with several others appearing on occasion. And these species have very much the same body form; significant morphological differences between them are largely in their feeding mechanisms, with each adapted to a distinctive diet. Their foods range from plankton to small bottom-dwelling shrimps, and from

Plate 27. Long-nosed butterflyfish, *Forcipiger flavissimus (lauwiliwili nukunuku ʻoiʻoi)*, make good use of their elongated snouts in probing for prey deep in reef crevices.

Plate 28. Ornate butterflyfish, *Chaetodon ornatissimus*, with insert showing nocturnal coloration.

Plate 29 Four-spot butterflyfish, *Chaetodon quadrimaculatus*

Plate 30. Masked butterflyfish, *Chaetodon lunula*.

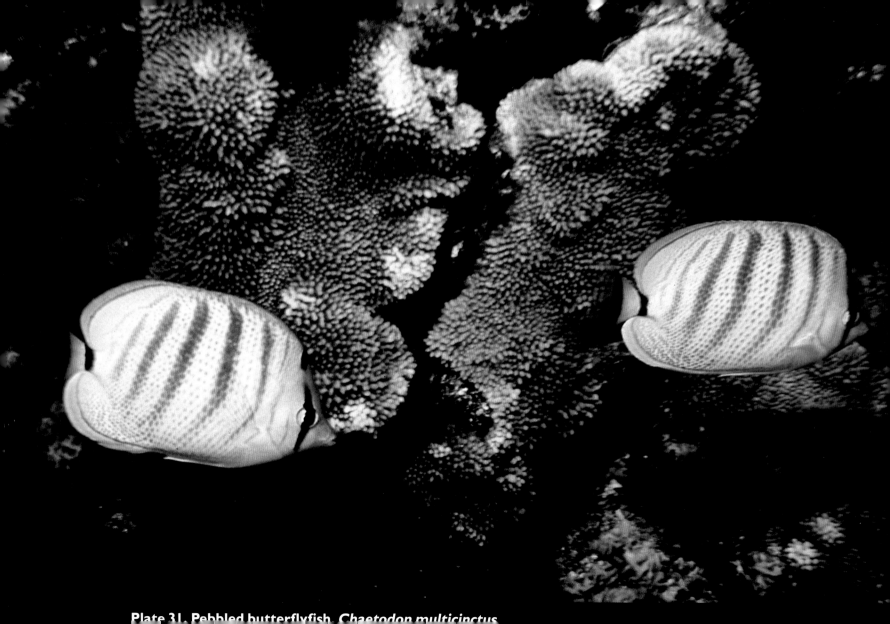

Plate 31. Pebbled butterflyfish, *Chaetodon multicinctus*.

worms to sea slugs and corals (22). Although some, such as *Chaetodon auriga*, take varied prey, most feed on a relatively narrow range of organisms, an extreme being *C. trifascialis*, which feeds on just one species of coral (38). Clearly the diversity of butterflyfishes is based on adaptive radiation of their feeding mechanisms to match the varied·feeding opportunities available on coral reefs. This situation could not have developed, however, without clear means to keep the species separated, and thus prevent interbreeding. Considering how similar they are otherwise, it seems likely that these fishes have achieved the required segregation through species recognition based largely on their distinctive, highly visible patterns of color (22).

The benefit at least many butterflyfishes gain from their distinctive visual displays apparently extends into the night, even though most of them are active primarily by day (22). This is implicit in nocturnal variations of their daytime color patterns, which are more visible in dim light (22). These variations tend to accentuate a contrast; for example, the diagonal orange bars that characterize *Chaetodon ornatissimus* during the day are bordered with black at night, thus increasing the contrast with their white background (Plate 28). Some species that do not change color at night have what seems to be effective contrast in their regular daytime patterns, for example the two white spots on black that are part of the coloration of *Chaetodon quadrimaculatus* (Plate 29) and the black bar through white on the head of *C. lunula* (Plate 30).

This apparent need for distinguishing features visible in dim light cannot be attributed to the fact that some of them feed at night. Although there are some nocturnal feeders among the butterflyfishes, for example *Chaetodon lunula*, at least some of the species with distinctive nocturnal colorations, like the vast majority of family members, feed strictly by day (22). Many butterflyfishes form lasting pairs (41), and highly visible nocturnal features could help them maintain contact through the night (22). On the other hand, among the butterflyfishes that form lasting pairs there are relatively drab species, for example *Chaetodon multicinctus* (Plate 31), which does not have highly contrasting nocturnal hues. It would appear, therefore, that butterflyfishes use their colorations in a number of ways.

Angelfishes

The angelfishes, family Pomacanthidae, were long considered among the butterflyfishes, but ichthyologists now regard them as distinct. Nevertheless, the two groups are much alike in general appearance, and most of what was said above about butterflyfishes also applies to angel-

Plate 32. Potter's angel, *Centropyge potteri.*

fishes. The potter's angel, *Centropyge potteri* (Plate 32), is the only angelfish numerous on shallow Hawaiian reefs, but it is among the most common fishes there. This species feeds mainly on filamentous algae and detritus that it scrapes from dead coral surfaces within small territories on the reef (22).

Damselfishes

The damselfishes, family Pomacentridae, are numerous on Hawaiian reefs, but so far as is known today, only two of the larger species—both members of the genus *Abudefduf*—have Hawaiian names: *A. abdominalis*, called *maomao*; and *A. sordidus*, called *kūpīpī*. The habits of these two are distinctive. *Maomao* are particularly abundant close to vertical faces of rocky reefs, where they aggregate to feed on plankton (primarily copepods) near the water's surface. *Kūpīpī*, on the other hand, are most numerous among crevices along edges of shallow rocky reefs, where they feed as individuals on a wide variety of bottom-dwelling organisms (both plants and animals) from reef surfaces (22).

Probably these two damselfishes were distinguished because they occur close to rocky shores and at up to 9 or 10 inches long (40) are large enough to be caught and eaten by people that fished there. In fact, chiefs are reported to have been fond of *maomao*, and a favored way to prepare *kūpīpī* for eating was to broil them in *ti* leaves after a full day exposed to hot sun (52). Furthermore, attention undoubtedly was drawn to the juveniles of both species because they are numerous in tide pools.

The other damselfishes seem to lack Hawaiian names; probably they were unimportant to Islanders because of their small size or relative inaccessibility. Their great abundance and activities in daylight, however, make them highly visible to modern scuba divers. The species are about equally divided between those that aggregate to feed on plankton above the reef, as does the *maomao*, and those that feed as individuals on bottom-dwelling organisms from reef surfaces, as does the *kūpīpī*.

While feeding above the reef, the plankton feeders form aggregations that can be related to the influence of predators. The very fact that they aggregate evidences increased risk of attack, because this behavior is widely considered a defense against most predators, which are thought to be confused by multiple targets (20). The threat of attack is also implicit in the distances above the reef at which the different species aggregate. Because larger fishes can swim faster than smaller ones, they should be able to feed farther above the reef and still make it back to shelter before threatening predators can get to them.

Plate 33. Damselfish, *Chromis agilis.*

Plate 34. Damselfish, *Chromis ovalis.*

Plate 35. Damselfish,
Stegastes fasciolatus.

Plate 36. Damselfish, *Plectroglyphidodon johnstonianus.*

This relation between size and feeding distance from the reef is evident in the distribution of the species of *Chromis* (22), which include all but one of the six damselfish species that feed on plankton above Hawaiian reefs (other than the *maomao*). The smallest, *C. vanderbilti* (maximum size about 3 inches), generally stays within a foot or two of the reef, while the two next in size, *C. agilis* (Plate 33) and *C. hanui* (maximum sizes about 4 to 5 inches), stay within 3 or 4 feet. And the two largest, *C. ovalis* (Plate 34) and *C. verater* (maximum sizes about 8 or 9 inches), may range 15 or more feet above the reef. The relatively large *maomao*, which is equal in size to or even larger than these last two, similarly ranges widely above the reef. Apparently the relatively large *C. ovalis* and *C. verater* did not get the attention of early Islanders, perhaps because they frequent the more offshore reefs, where they are relatively inaccessible.

The five bottom-feeding damselfish species, including the *kūpīpī*, establish well-defined territories on the reef. Although all but the *kūpīpī* are less than about 5 inches long, they defend their territories vigorously, often driving off intruders many times their own size. They feed strictly by day and their diets are distinctive. One of them is *Stegastes fasciolatus* (Plate 35), a plant eater, and one of the most widespread and numerous of Hawaiian reef fishes. Another is *Plectroglyphidodon johnstonianus*

(Plate 36), which is distributed in close association with the corals on which it feeds. Others include *P. imparipennis* and *P. sindonis*, both of which live in surge-swept water only a few feet deep—the former close to basaltic reefs, the latter around the bases of basaltic boulders (22).

Hawkfishes

The hawkfishes, family Cirrhitidae, include three small fishes distinguished by Hawaiians as different forms of *pilikoʻa* (coral clinging): *Cirrhitops fasciatus* (Plate 37), *Paracirrhites arcatus* (Plate 38), and *P. forsteri* (Plate 39). They are relatively small fishes, most less than 6 inches long, that perch in full view on reef formations during the day. The habits of each are distinctive. *Cirrhitops fasciatus*, known as *oʻopu pilikoʻa* (52), is the most versatile. This fish occurs on a variety of reef surfaces and feeds during both day and night on many kinds of benthic organisms, in particular crabs and shrimps (22). Most specialized is *P. arcatus*, which usually is perched on the coral *Pocillopora meandrina* and feeds only by day—largely on crabs that live between the branches of this coral (22).

The habits of *P. forsteri*, known as *hilu pilikoʻa*, present a paradox. This predator feeds by day, mainly on smaller fishes that come within range of a sudden rush

**Plate 37. Hawkfish,
Cirrhitops fasciatus
(o'opu piliko'a).**

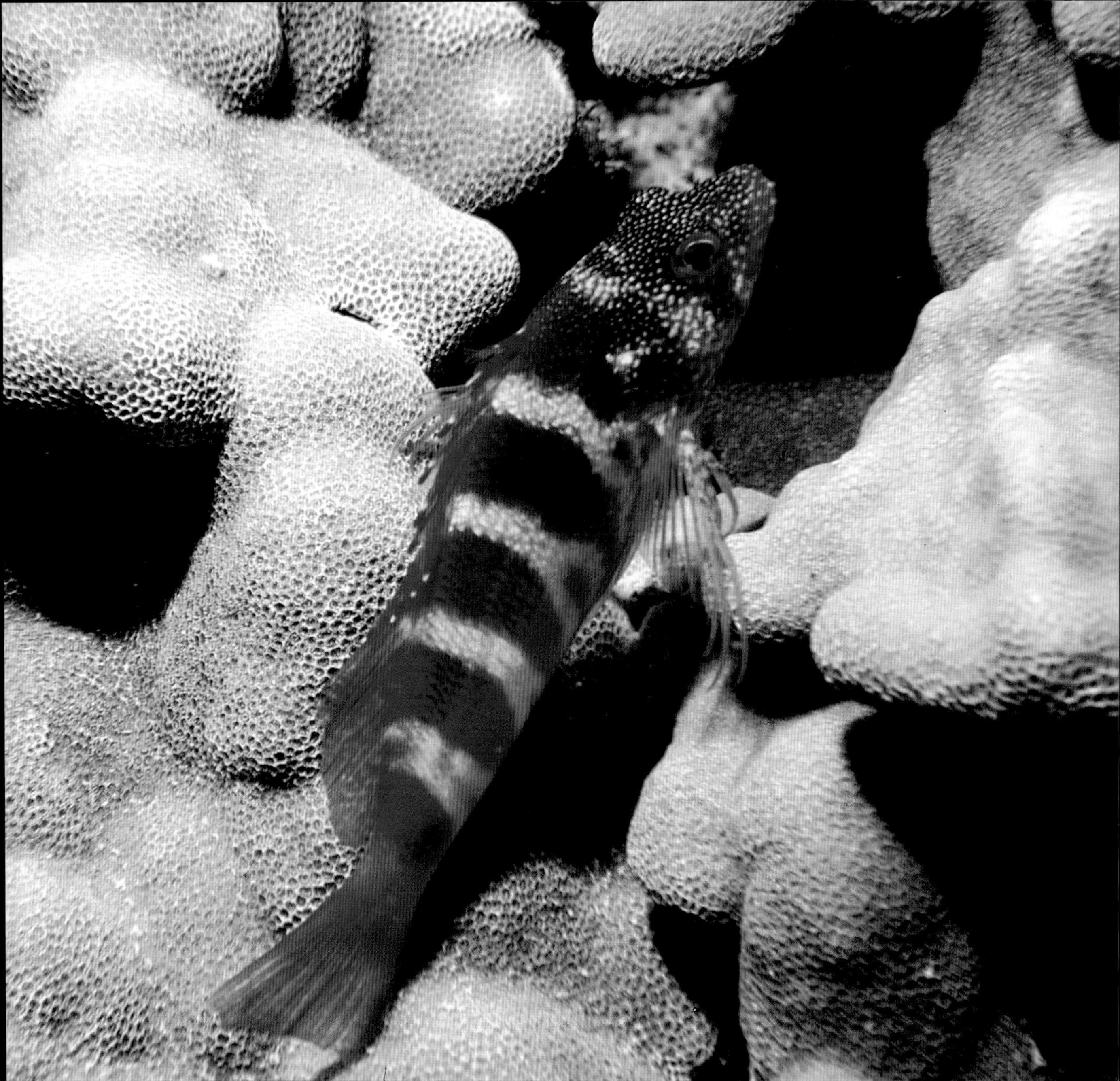

Plate 38. Hawkfish, *Paracirrhites arcatus (piliko'a)*.

Plate 39. Hawkfish, *Paracirrhites forsteri* (hilu pilikoʻa).

Plate 40. Hawkfish, *Cirrhites pinnulatus* **(po'opa'a).**

from its perch on the reef. Many reef predators feed this way, but except for *P. forsteri* they are cryptic fishes that blend into their surroundings and depend on going unnoticed to ambush prey. Far from being cryptic, this hawkfish is conspicuous, at least to human eyes, because of highly visible coloration (Plate 39). The question is, therefore, how can this predator be a successful ambusher when elements of its coloration are so readily seen? The answer may be that *hilu piliko'a* actually finds prey among small fishes that approach to investigate its conspicuous features. Certainly many fishes are attracted to conspicuous objects on the sea floor—one need only place a small shiny artifact on the bottom to demonstrate this. Conceivably this could be an effective way to capture prey so long as its use among predators is limited (22).

Another type of hawkfish prominent on Hawaiian reefs is *Cirrhites pinnulatus* (Plate 40), called by Hawaiians *po'opa'a* (stubborn). Unlike the readily seen *piliko'a*, this is a nocturnal fish that tends to stay hidden among the coral during the day. It grows larger than the *piliko'a*, attaining lengths of about 10 inches, and probably for this reason it alone among the hawkfishes has long been considered food. Opinions differed as to its edibility, however, and although some considered it delicious, others held it in some disdain. This second opinion is evident in the old expression: "*Hōkai ua lawai'a o ka kai papa'u, he po'opa'a ka i'a e ho'i ai,*" which translates as, "The fisherman that fools around in shallow water takes home a *po'opa'a* fish" (52).

Mullets

The mullet that regularly occurs in the vicinity of Hawaiian reefs is *Chaenomugil leuciscus* (Plate 41), called *uouoa* by early Islanders. This species tends to occur in marine habitats along open shores, whereas the other mullet native to the Islands, *Mugil cephalus*, called *'ama 'ama*, is more typical of brackish water (14). The *uouoa* grow to about 18 inches long and were a favored food in early times. Occasionally, however, an Islander who had eaten this fish was afflicted with nightmares, like those caused by eating certain of the goatfishes (see above). The condition, like the similar condition caused by goatfishes, was attributed to the murder of Pahulu, chief of ghosts. Before eating a *uouoa*, therefore, one was advised to throw away one of its bones and say, "Here is your share, O Pahulu" (52).

Wrasses

The colorful wrasses are among the more distinctive fishes on Hawaiian reefs. They include fishes of all shapes and sizes, although most are less than a foot long. There

61

Plate 41. Mullet, *Chaenomugil leuciscus (uouoa)*.

has long been uncertainty of the number of wrasse species that inhabit Hawaiian reefs. At present they are numbered at 42 (40), which is fewer by one-third the number recognized 30 years ago. The difficulty has been that wrasse species generally include two or more distinct forms: coloration, especially, differs with age and sex. To further complicate matters, it is widespread in this family, probably universal, that individuals change sex at some point during their lives (42). For these reasons, many species contain two or more forms each long thought to be distinct species.

Wrasses swim with a characteristic rowing motion of their pectoral fins, and only when sudden speed is needed do they use the sweeping tail strokes that propel most other fishes. They have small mouths, with sharp, pointed teeth, and carry in their throats heavy bones that crush the shelled animals on which most of them prey. All the wrasses restrict their activity to daylight; after dark they rest under cover on the reef or under the sand (14).

A number of the more prominent wrasses were known to early Islanders as varieties of *hīnālea*. *Thalassoma duperrey* (Plate 42), called *hīnālea lauwili*, occurs only in Hawaiian waters, where it is perhaps the most ubiquitous of the reef fishes. Other varieties of *hīnālea* include *Thalassoma ballieui*, called *hīnālea luahine* (old-woman *hinalea*), and *Gomphosus varius* (Plate 43), called *hīnālea nuku 'i'iwi* (*hīnālea* with a beak like a bird).

Hawaiians valued *hīnālea* as food and kept them in pools so as to be available when needed. Often these fishes were eaten when drinking *'awa* because they were considered to provide a good aftertaste (52). In preparing them as the major ingredient of *i'a ho'omelu*, a favorite dish, *hīnālea* were allowed to partially decompose before being seasoned with *kukui* nuts and chili peppers. Not surprisingly, the preparation had a strong, foul odor, which led to the phrase *ipu kai hīnālea* (dish of *hīnālea* sauce) being applied to someone with unpleasant breath (39).

Hīnālea also had religious significance. They were offered to the gods in one ceremony to bring on pregnancy (52). The *hīnālea nuku 'i'iwi* was used by *kāhuna* as a *pani*, which is a bit of food given to close a period of medical treatment. The affliction treated was mental illness, and this particular fish was appropriate because a second name for the species, *hīnālea 'akilolo*, is pertinent (*'aki*, to nibble; *lolo*, brain) (52).

Among other prominent wrasses are several gaily hued species of the genus *Coris*, which were recognized by ancient Hawaiians as varieties of *hilu*, a word meaning "well behaved." It was said that women who craved this fish during their pregnancy would give birth to quiet, dig-

**Plate 42. Saddle wrasse,
Thalassoma duperrey
(hīnālea lauwili).**

Plate 43. Bird wrasse, *Gomphosus varius* (hīnālea nuku ʻiʻwi or hīnālea ʻakilolo).

Plate 44. Eight-lined wrasse, *Pseudocheilinus octotaenia*.

Plate 45. Cleaner wrasse, *Labroides phthirophagus*, attending damselfish, *Chromis agilis*.

nified children (52). In addition, certain *hilu* were considered gods who could assume human form at will (52). Still other prominent wrasses include *Halichoeres ornatissimus*, called *lā'ō* (sugarcane leaf); *Anampses cuvier*, called *'ōpule*; *Bodianus bilunulatus*, called *'a'awa*; *Cheilio inermis*, called *kūpou*; and *Pseudocheilinus octotaenia* (Plate 44). Truly this is a varied group.

One little wrasse that is not known to have attracted the attention of ancient Hawaiians has excited the interest of some present-day Islanders. This is *Labroides phthirophagus* (Plate 45), which does not exceed a length of more than a few inches and has the habit of picking external parasites off the bodies of other fishes. Generally only a few of them inhabit a given area, and these individuals occur at well-defined locations recognized to be "cleaning stations." The other fishes on the reef know the location of these stations and swim there when they need their bodies cleansed of parasites. Upon arriving at a cleaning station, the visitors generally pose motionless in a characteristic fashion. Their soliciting attitude attracts the cleaner, which approaches them, inspects their bodies, and then may proceed to pick off the irritating parasites. Sometimes many fishes hover together at a cleaning station, all waiting to have their parasites removed by the little cleaner (33). Frequently a diver is surprised to see hovering near the coral a large offshore species not normally seen on the shallower reefs, and a closer look shows that it is visiting a cleaning station.

Parrotfishes

The colorful parrotfishes, of the family Scaridae, are another group especially characteristic of coral reefs. Called *uhu* by Hawaiians, they are closely related to the wrasses, which they resemble. Generally these fishes are larger than wrasses, however, with members of some species growing to about 2 feet long. Perhaps their most distinctive feature is a parrotlike beak, formed by the fusion of their teeth. This feature, combined with brilliant hues in many species, makes the parrotfishes a well-named group.

Using their heavy beak, parrotfishes scrape algae off the surfaces of rocks and dead coral, an activity that scrapes away surface layers of the coral rock as well. After this material is ground to a fine powder by bones in the parrotfish's throat, it passes on through the digestive tract and finally is deposited on the sea floor. It has been suggested that much of the fine coral sand on a coral reef has passed through the guts of parrotfishes (2). These animals seem to be defecating much of the time, a fact that probably led to Hawaiians calling one form *uhu pālukaluka* (*uhu* with loose bowels).

Parrotfishes are active only in daylight. At night they rest among the rocks and coral on the reef, and at that time many of them secrete a mucous envelope about themselves (Plates 46 and 47). It has been suggested that these mucous coverings protect them from large nocturnal predators, such as moray eels (56). They may be more important, however, as protection from very small predaceous crustaceans, notably isopods, which despite being less than an inch long can do serious, even lethal, damage to fishes that rest on the reef at night (48).

Uhu have long been favorites of Islanders. Many Hawaiian names refer to specific forms among these fishes, but are difficult to associate with species known today. Even some of the names scientists use for several of them are uncertain. The main problem is that, as with the wrasses, usually each species of parrotfish has several forms, with distinctions being related to age and sex (Plate 48). In addition, the differences are clouded by the fact that, as with wrasses, some individuals, perhaps all of them, change sex at some time during their lives (43).

Some distinctive forms nevertheless seem identifiable among the names used by early Islanders. *Uhu ʻāhiuhiu* (untamed *uhu*), described as a large blue species (52), probably is the large male of *Scarus perspicillatus* (Plate 49); *uhu pālukaluka*, described as reddish brown on its upper body and bright red on its lower (52), is probably the adult female of *Scarus rubroviolaceus;* and *uhu ʻele-ʻele* (dark *uhu*), described as a large green fish (52), may be the adult male of *Scarus rubroviolaceus*.

The prominence of *uhu* among Hawaiian fishes is reflected in their frequent reference in Island lore. One legendary *uhu* was the fish-god Uhu-mākaʻikaʻi (roving, sight-seeing *uhu*). It is told that when very young, Uhŭ-mākaʻikaʻi was caught by a fisherman who raised him to great size in captivity. When fully grown, Uhu-mākaʻi-kaʻi was released to the sea, but thereafter answered his master's bidding to drive vast numbers of fishes up onto the shore. In this way, the people living along the coast between Makapuʻu and Kualoa on Oʻahu were regularly supplied with an abundance of food (12). Despite this service to the people, Uhu-mākaʻikaʻi was hunted by the legendary hero Kawelo. Taking to sea in a canoe, Kawelo sought his quarry for two days off the Waiʻanae coast. Finally Uhu-mākaʻikaʻi appeared, his approach heralded by gathering storm clouds. Kawelo set his net, entrapping the mighty fish-god, and a wild battle ensued. Uhu-mākaʻikaʻi could not free himself from the net, and Kawelo could not bring him in, so the two were locked together as the canoe was towed far from land. The struggle continued north as far as the island of Kauaʻi, then back to Oʻahu. At last, with help from other Islanders, Kawelo subdued and then killed the great *uhu* at Waikīkī (44).

Plate 46. Parrotfish, *Scarus psittacus* (uhu), in a mucous envelope at night.

Plate 47 Parrotfishes, _Scarus dubius (left)_ and _S. sordidus (right)_, at rest in mucous envelopes at night.

Plate 48. Parrotfish, _Scarus sordidus._ Females in foreground, lone male in background.

Plate 49. Parrotfish, *Scarus perspicillatus*, being cleaned about head by *Labroides phthirophagus*.

In the old days, fishermen believed that the way they saw *uhu* behaving at sea told them how their wives were behaving at home. Thus, when *uhu* frolicked in the water, a fisherman knew that his wife was guilty of improper levity at home. If two *uhu* were seen rubbing their snouts together, the fisherman knew it was time to stow his gear and return home, where an unfaithful wife needed to be punished (52).

Blennies

Hawaiian blennies, family Blenniidae, were recognized by early Islanders as various forms of *pao'o*. Each has a pair of fins far forward under the throat that prop them up in a characteristic pose while at rest on rocks or coral. They are elongated fishes that swim with exaggerated undulations of the body. The largest of them is no more than about 7 inches long, but they are among the most numerous fishes in tide pools and shallow water along rocky shores (14).

The rockskipper, *Istiblennius zebra*, probably is the fish Hawaiians called *pao'o lēhei* (leaping *pao'o*). It inhabits tide pools and characteristically leaps from pool to pool in a way that demonstrates familiarity with the relative positions of pools in its home area (50). Probably it is a *pao'o* of this species that describes itself to others in this old chant:

This is *pao'o, pao'o*
That rogue, that mischief maker
That rests on the *lipoa* seaweed.
A nibble here, a nibble there.
I leap, I jump,
I leap into the large sea pools,
I leap into the small sea pools,
Poking this, taking that. . . . (52)

Islanders fishing from rocky shores frequently took these blennies from the pools and used them for bait and in the process often would pop one into their mouths. These fish were not eaten raw once they had died, however, because then they have a bitter taste (52).

Although most blennies live in shallow water near shore, several species inhabit the deeper reefs seaward. One of these, *Exallias brevis* (Plate 50), called *pao'o kauila*, has perhaps the most striking coloration among Hawaiian blennies. Like most other family members, *E. brevis* has movable comblike teeth, which it uses to scrape certain hard surfaces on the seabed. But whereas most others scrape fine plants and organic deposits from surfaces of rocks and dead coral, this species scrapes coral tissue and mucus from the surfaces of living corals (22).

Two other family members that occur in deeper water have highly exceptional feeding habits. These are the saber-tooth blennies, *Plagiotremus ewaensis* and *P. gosli-*

Plate 50. Blenny,
Exallius brevis
(pao'o kauila).

nei. Although neither grows to more than a few inches long, they attack other fishes many times their own size. Striking from a hovering position above the reef, they usually attack the larger fishes from below or behind. Upon contact, the startled victim bolts forward and swims away, having lost to the blenny some of its body mucus and perhaps skin fragments. Saber-tooth blennies owe their name to the pair of fanglike teeth they carry in their lower jaw. These teeth are not used in feeding, however, but perhaps in territorial conflicts. When not hovering above the reef, the saber-tooth blennies occupy abandoned mollusk shells or worm tubes embedded in the rocks or coral (9, 21).

Gobies

The gobies, known to early Hawaiians as various forms of *'o'opu,* constitute the family Gobiidae. They include an assortment of small fishes, many of them less than an inch long even when fully grown. Because these fishes typically sit motionless on substrata colored much like themselves, they often go unnoticed by the casual observer. Some, the *'o'opu wai,* live in Hawaii's freshwater streams, and it is these that are most often mentioned in Island lore. Our interest here, however, is with those living in the sea, the *'o'opu kai.* The saltwater gobies inhabit a variety of habitats, from deeper waters on the reef to tide pools along the shore.

The gobies are unique among Hawaiian fishes in that the pair of fins on their underside are fused together to form a sucking disc. This structure effectively grasps the sea floor, which the fish finds particularly helpful in maintaining position in turbulent water. The goby *Bathygobius fuscus,* called *'ōhune,* probably is the most abundant fish in Island tide pools (14).

Surgeonfishes

Probably more of the fishes that swim over Hawaiian reefs belong to the surgeonfish family Acanthuridae than to any other (Plate 51). These colorful animals, which range in length from about 7 inches to over 2 feet, owe their name to the knifelike spines that each carries on the base of its tail. Most surgeonfishes have a single sharp spine on either side that folds into a sheath of skin; the fish erects these spines when threatened and with them can seriously injure an unwary fisherman. Other surgeonfishes carry on each side a number of fixed spines, which are blunt in comparison to the single, folding type.

The various Hawaiian reef habitats each have a characteristic assemblage of surgeonfish species (28). Where waves crash against the reef, and the water often is a swirl

Plate 51. The seven species that dominate this typical assemblage of Hawaiian reef fishes are all surgeonfishes.

Plate 52. Surgeonfish, *Acanthurus leucopareius* **(māikoiko).**

Plate 53. Brown tang, *Acanthurus nigrofuscus (māʻiʻiʻi).*

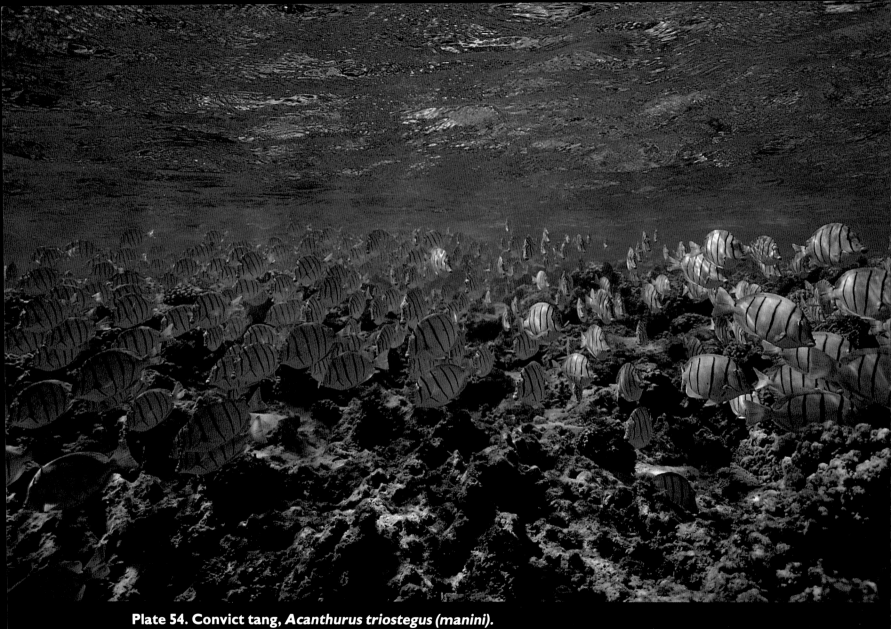

Plate 54. Convict tang, *Acanthurus triostegus (manini).*

Plate 55. Gold-eye tang, *Ctenochaetus strigosus (kole)*.

Plate 56. Yellow tang, *Zebrasoma flavescens* (lau'īpala).

Plate 57. Orange-spine unicornfish, *Naso lituratus (kala),* at rest on coral at night, with small shrimp, probably a cleaner, on its lower jaw.

Plate 58. Unicorn tang, *Naso unicornis (kala)*, at rest at night.

of bubbles and turbulence, the surgeonfishes present usually include *Acanthurus leucopareius*, called *māikoiko* (Plate 52); *A. achilles*, called *pāku'iku'i*; and *A. guttatus*, called *api*. Where a submerged lava flow is dotted with small, isolated coral heads, but is not yet encrusted with other sea life, typically a dominant surgeonfish is *A. nigrofuscus* (Plate 53). Where the sea floor immediately below the surge zone is overgrown with corals, usually the dominant surgeonfishes include *Acanthurus triostegus* (Plate 54), called *manini*; *Ctenochaetus strigosus* (Plate 55), called *kole*; *Zebrasoma flavescens* (Plate 56), called *lau'īpala*; and *Naso lituratus* (Plate 57), called *kala*. And where reefs in water deeper than about 30 feet are interspersed with patches of sand, the dominant surgeonfishes often included *Acanthurus dussumieri*, called *palani*; *A. xanthopterus*, called *pualu*; and *A. olivaceus*, called *na'ena'e*.

All those mentioned so far are bottom feeders; most, like the *manini*, crop seaweeds from hard substrata, but others, like the *na'ena'e*, sift through sand for tiny food items that have accumulated there. A few surgeonfishes find their food in the water above the reef: these include *Acanthurus thompsoni* and *Naso hexacanthus*, which feed mostly on tiny animals that drift as plankton in open waters (28). All of this feeding occurs during the day; at night the surgeonfishes rest on or close to the reef (Plates 57 and 58).

The surgeonfishes have long been a favorite food of Hawaiians, despite the fact that smaller species, like the *manini*, do not carry much flesh. Furthermore, many have a strong, unpleasant odor, especially some of the larger species, like the *palani*. An old Hawaiian tale recounts how the *palani* acquired its odor: Once, lost at sea, the legendary Ke'emalu remembered her ancestor among the surgeonfishes, a god named Palani nui maha-o'o. She called to him for aid, and the great fish soon appeared to carry her shoreward on his back. Midway through the journey, Ke'emalu was overcome by the strong need to urinate. Unable to control herself, she urinated on her ancestor's back, an act which understandably infuriated the fish-god. He immediately threw Ke'emalu into the sea, leaving her to swim ashore on her own, but the strong, unpleasant odor has persisted to the present day in this species of surgeonfish (52).

Moorish Idol

The moorish idol, *Zanclus cornutus* (Plate 59), one of the most graceful and distinctively beautiful species in the sea, is closely related to the surgeonfishes, and some ichthyologists consider it to be a member of that family. However, it lacks the spines on the base of the tail fin, which are characteristic of the surgeonfishes, and so is considered by most ichthyologists to represent a family of

Plate 59. Moorish idol, *Zanclus cornutus (kihikihi)*.

its own, the Zanclidae. It grows to about 9 inches long and was called by Hawaiians *kihikihi* (angular). Usually swimming among the corals and rocks in groups of four to six or so individuals, the *kihikihi* probes with its long snout in reef crevices and narrow depressions, mainly for sponges (22).

Flounders

The flounder most often seen on Hawaiian reefs is *Bothus mancus* (Plate 60), known to Islanders as *pāki'i*. It attains a length of about 14 inches (40), but generally goes unnoticed even when fully exposed on the reef. This is because it lies motionless, flush against the reef, and assumes a coloration that matches the surroundings. It is even more difficult to see when lying under a covering of sand, which is a frequent habit. The *pāki'i* preys on smaller fishes during the day (22), so its cryptic features allow it to go unseen and ambush unsuspecting prey.

Triggerfishes and Filefishes

Triggerfishes, family Balistidae, are distinctive, slow-moving creatures that appear harmless. The fact is, however, that the relatively small mouths of most are equipped with exceptionally strong teeth and jaws that can seriously injure a careless fisherman. These features are adaptations to diets of hard-shelled organisms, like sea urchins.

Triggerfishes, most of which attain lengths of between 7 and 12 inches, owe their name to the mechanism that locks upright the long front spine of their dorsal fin. When thus positioned, the spine cannot be depressed until the smaller second spine, the trigger, is released. These fishes are served well by this structure when threatened, as they dive into narrow crevices in the reef and wedge themselves in by locking their spine erect.

To early Hawaiians, the different triggerfishes were various types of *humuhumu*. Two similar species, *Rhinecanthus rectangulus* (Hawaii's state fish) and *R. aculeatus*, are well known in song as *humuhumunukunuku-āpua'a* (*humuhumu* with a snout like a pig). Others include *Melichthys niger*, called *humuhumu 'ele'ele* (dark *humuhumu*); *M. vidua*, called *humuhumu hi'u kole* (red-tailed *humuhumu*); and *Sufflamen bursa*, known as *humuhumu umauma lei* (*humuhumu* with leis on its chest) (39).

The closely related filefishes are considered by some ichthyologists to constitute a separate family, the Monacanthidae. They differ from the triggerfishes by the position of the large first dorsal spine, which is farther forward—over the eyes in filefishes, as compared to behind

Plate 60. Flounder, *Bothus mancus* (pāki‘i).

Plate 61. Filefish, *Pervagor spilosoma* ('ō'ili 'uwī'uwī).

the eyes in triggerfishes. Additionally, filefishes have a soft velvety body surface, in contrast to the hard, almost armorlike encasement of triggerfishes.

Early Islanders knew several kinds of filefishes as different forms of *'ō'ili* (to make an appearance). *Pervagor spilosoma* (Plate 61), called *'ō'ili 'uwī'uwī* (squealing *'ō'ili*), is a relatively common species that does not exceed a length of about 5 inches. Occasionally this fish appears in nearshore areas in great numbers, with literally millions washing up onto the beaches. In ancient days, this event was thought to foretell the death of a high chief (52). *'Ō'ili 'uwī'uwī* have never been valued as food, but because their flesh is very oily ancient Hawaiians regularly burned them as fuel.

Boxfishes

The boxfishes, family Ostraciontidae, are peculiar creatures. The body of each is encased in a solid bony box, so that swimming movements are confined to the fins and tail; understandably, they are not strong swimmers. Although seemingly vulnerable to predators, boxfishes show little concern when closely approached by a diver. Because at least some boxfishes secrete a poisonous substance from their skin (14), it may be that predators reject them as prey.

The most common boxfish in Hawaii is *Ostracion meleagris*, known as *pahu* (box). Most *pahu* are dark with white spots, but large males are brilliantly hued with yellow and blue (Plate 62). The striking appearance of this fish, and the ease with which it is captured, make the *pahu* a tempting target for those seeking aquarium specimens; however, this is a temptation to be resisted, because its poisonous secretions will kill other fishes with which it is confined.

Pufferfishes

The pufferfishes include three distinct types: the balloonfishes (Plate 63), which constitute the family Tetraodontidae; the sharpback puffers, which are considered by some to represent a family distinct from the above, the Canthigasteridae; and the spiny puffers, or porcupinefishes (Plate 64), which constitute the family Diodontidae. Some balloonfishes grow to about 2 feet long, and some of the spiny puffers attain a comparable size, but the maximum length of sharpback puffers is only about 5 inches (14). All pufferfishes have sharp beaks and powerful jaws. These structures, which can seriously injure humans, are adaptations for feeding on hard-shelled organisms, like sea urchins and mollusks.

In old Hawaii, most puffers were known, collectively, as

Plate 62. Boxfish,
Ostracion meleagris
(pahu).

Plate 63. Balloonfish, *Arothron meleagris* **('o'opu hue).**

Plate 64. Porcupinefish, *Diodon hystrix (kōkala)*.

'o'opu hue (stomach like a gourd), or kēkē (pot-bellied). The name refers to their most outstanding characteristic: an ability to inflate themselves like a balloon by swallowing water or air. Another characteristic of these fishes presents a paradox: although the puffers are among the most poisonous of all marine animals, many of them are highly prized as food. Certain internal organs and the skin contain a potent nerve poison. Although the flesh is edible, a human who eats a piece that has been contaminated during preparation by poison from an adjacent organ has better than a 60 percent chance of a painful death (15).

Sea Turtle

There is only one species of sea turtle common on Hawaiian reefs, but this one, the green turtle, Chelonia mydus (Plate 65), is abundant throughout the archipelago (1). Called honu by early Islanders, green turtles were a highly esteemed food in the old days, but their numbers were effectively conserved because they were reserved for royalty (29). Honu were caught several ways. One common method was to harpoon them from a rocky shore; another was to snare them using a pair of hooks fastened to a flat stone (7). Probably threats from humans have kept honu off the beaches of the major islands since early times. These animals come ashore to bask on islands in the northwestern part of the archipelago that were un-known to early Hawaiians, but they do not do this on the long-inhabited major Hawaiian Islands (1). Apparently basking ashore, a rare behavior among marine turtles, is inhibited by contact with humans.

Green turtles establish what may be lifelong residences in coastal areas where there are beds of the marine vegetation that is their food and places that serve as shelter when they are at rest (1). These residences occur throughout the archipelago, from the island of Hawai'i to tiny Kure atoll, but when time comes to breed virtually all honu migrate to certain islands at French Frigate Shoals, in the center of the archipelago. This is a trip that adult males may make each year, but one that females make less often (1).

Clearly, conditions for nesting are favorable on the low sandy islands at French Frigate Shoals. Not only are these small islands composed of materials suitable for digging, but they are also remote from humans and other predators that would threaten the eggs. Similar conditions exist at other islands in the northwestern part of the archipelago, and in fact some nesting occurs at several of them. There has also been breeding at some beaches on the major islands in years past, for example at Polihua Beach on Lāna'i. But at the present time over 90 percent of all breeding by Hawaiian green turtles occurs at French Frigate Shoals (1).

Apparently each breeding turtle returns to the site of its

Plate 65. Green turtle, *Chelonia mydus (honu)*.

birth. They arrive in the shallow waters off the nesting islands during April and for the next two months are busy with courtship and then mating. The females start nesting during mid-May, with most doing so in June or July and very few after that. They come out of the water and begin digging the pits that will be their nests late in the afternoon, but do not lay eggs until after dark. The number of eggs laid and then buried by each turtle averages about 100. These hatch about two months later, leaving the hatchlings to struggle up through about 2 feet of sand to reach the surface. They emerge from the sand at night, usually shortly after sunset, and then head for the water. They are only about 2 inches long (shell length) at this time, and a number of them fall prey to ghost crabs, *Ocypode ceratophthalmus*, near the water's edge. Only relatively few are taken, however, compared to the numbers of green-turtle hatchlings taken by sea birds elsewhere in the world where the trip to the water is made in daylight (1).

After the hatchlings enter the sea they are not seen again until they appear at locations near shore throughout the archipelago, and by this time their shells have grown to about 14 inches long (1). Nothing is known of their early lives in the open ocean, but once back in coastal waters they settle in the areas where, except for breeding migrations as adults, they will spend the rest of their lives (1).

Monk Seal

Hawaiian monk seals, *Monachus schauinslandi* (Plate 66), have long been among the rarest and least known of marine mammals. They inhabit the low sandy islands and atolls that are the northwestern part of the archipelago and fare poorly when in contact with humans. Probably because they evolved where all threats were in the sea, monk seals seem oblivious to danger when ashore and show little concern when humans approach. This trusting nature was exploited by sealers during the 1800s, and the species was headed toward extinction before conservationists intervened early during the present century. Salvation of the monk seal and other fragile forms clinging to existence on the northwestern Hawaiian Islands came when federal and state law designated all of that area a refuge for wildlife. The monk seal has since inceased in numbers, with breeding populations from Nihoa to Kure atoll (18), and under continued protection as an endangered species its future appears secure, at least for the moment.

Monk seals grow to a large size—more than 8 feet in length and over 600 pounds in weight (32)—which probably is why they have few natural enemies. Sharks are a threat, particularly the tiger shark, *Galeocerdo cuvier*

Plate 66. Monk seal, *Monachus schauinslandi.*

(26), but a greater danger may be entanglement in fragments of fishing nets and other drifting debris—a common and sometimes fatal experience (17, 18). Sometimes female monk seals are mobbed in nearshore waters by numbers of males attempting to mate, and some of them die from injuries received (26).

Monk seals on shore spend most of the time basking on the sand, and only infrequently do they reveal how awkward they are out of water. Their clumsy undulations in moving about on land, however, contrast sharply with their fluid movements in the sea. Nevertheless, although they have clearly evolved as aquatic animals, the need to give birth and nurse young on land (32) ties them to their island homes. They also remain ashore for most of the nine or so days that it takes them to shed hair during their annual molt (27).

Monk seals feed mainly on fishes and cephalopods (32) and must strongly affect the populations of these prey close to their home beaches. This seemed the case during a study of reef fishes at Laysan Island, where reef caves near shore lacked the concentrations of soldierfishes, *Myripristis* spp., and other nocturnal species that generally are numerous in places remote from humans. One wonders whether tropical reef fishes are particularly vulnerable to monk seals. They experienced little or no contact with seals during their evolution and so may lack an effective defense against these predators. Tropical seals are rare. There are only three species of pinnepeds adapted to tropical conditions, all of them monk seals (i.e., of the genus *Monachus*), and they have extremely limited distributions. In addition to the Hawaiian species, there is one in the Mediterranean and another (which may now be extinct) in the Caribbean. Otherwise, seals have always been animals of temperate latitudes (46).

If the food needs of large monk-seal colonies exceed the numbers of prey immediately available, which seems probable, this would explain why these seals regularly spend weeks and even months away from their home beaches. It remains unknown how far they range during these extended forays, but when they return their bodies often are covered with barnacles and algae (49). It seems that they have access to extensive feeding grounds. Hawaiian monk seals live on the eroded remains of what once were much larger islands, and the submerged crests and slopes of these ancient structures are richly populated by potential prey (24, 55). Reefs abound over these broad areas, and monk seals, which can dive deeper than 500 feet (47), are capable of getting to most of them.

The
Invertebrates

Animals
without backbones

Plate 67 Stony corals, most of them forms of _Porites lobata_, dominate this Hawaiian reef.

Stony Corals

The most visible forms of life on Hawaiian reefs are stony corals (Plate 67), which biologists classify as the Scleractinia, a major component of the phylum Cnidaria. Their classification in this phylum of animals, which also includes the sea anemones and jellyfishes, is based on a basic body form that is essentially a sac with a single opening surrounded by tentacles. The sac serves as a stomach, while the opening serves for both ingesting food and eliminating wastes. The bodies of corals, called polyps, are elongate cylinders that attach to the seabed. In this respect they are similar to anemones, but different from jellyfishes, whose saclike bodies, called medusae, tend to be bell-shaped and swim freely in the water. Polyps of corals that dominate tropical reefs differ from anemones, however, in that they are small and clustered, whereas anemone polyps are relatively large and solitary. Although the bodies of the various Cnidaria take many different forms, all are armed with stinging cells, called nematocysts, which they carry on their tentacles. The nematocysts stun prey caught by the tentacles, making them more readily carried to the mouth. Although in some cnidarians, particularly among jellyfishes, the nematocysts are potent enough to painfully wound humans, generally only tiny prey are threatened.

Coral polyps that build reefs in tropical seas grow together as colonies, encased except for mouth and tentacles in a limestone skeleton that they secrete. The polyps are joined in these colonies not only by fusion of their stony skeletons, but also by a thin layer of living tissue that lies over the skeleton. The colony grows as the polyps multiply, one budding from another, with succeeding generations building on the skeletons of their predecessors. This growth produces highly variable structures, depending on the species and environmental conditions. Formations constructed by species of *Porites*, for example, may be massive (Plate 67), branching (Plate 4), leaflike (Plate 12), or encrusting (Plate 40), while species of *Pocillopora* grow as isolated branching heads (Plate 53).

The structures produced by reef-building corals are frameworks within which complex interactions among animals and plants produce what we see as coral-reef communities. Among the more important of these interactions are between the coral polyps and simple, single-cell algae called zooxanthellae. The zooxanthellae live within the coral's tissues and give to the corals their hues of brown, yellow, pink, and blue. Both corals and zooxanthellae benefit from this relationship, making it an example of what is known as symbiosis. The corals assimilate nutrients that the zooxanthellae produce through photosynthesis (the process by which virtually all plants convert sunlight into energy), while the zooxanthellae are in turn nourished by metabolic by-products of the corals

(36). The importance of this relationship to reef-building corals is evident in that they live only where the zooxanthellae in their tissues can get the sunlight needed for photosynthesis. This limitation generally precludes development of coral reefs at depths below about 180 feet, even in the clearest water (3).

Despite their dependence on symbiotic algae for energy, reef-building corals generally obtain most of their nourishment at night when their tentacles reach out from expanded polyps and capture small zooplankters. This feeding is much reduced during the day, however, when generally the polyps are contracted within their limestone encasements.

Not all stony corals build reefs or live in sunlight. An example is *Tubastrea coccinea* (Plate 68), a shallow-water representative of what is primarily a deep-water family, the Dendrophyllidae. This species forms small colonies in caves and under ledges, showing an attraction to shadows that probably reflects its deep-water heritage. With a history of living out of the sunlight, *T. coccinea* lacks the symbiotic zooxanthellae that are characteristic of reef-building corals. This means it must supply itself with all its nourishment, but it also means that it lives where there is no competition for space from corals that depénd on sunlight-dependent zooxanthellae (36).

In old Hawaii, stony corals, as a group, were known as *ko'a*. This also was the name given to fishing shrines, perhaps because these were so often made of coral skeletons. Although living corals are variably hued, after death their skeletons are white. This made coral rocks highly visible at night and was responsible for their widespread use as trail markers.

Mollusks

A wide variety of creatures is included among the mollusks, and many are prominent on Hawaiian reefs. Although the most visible feature of most is their shell, this is reduced to a rudiment in some species and is entirely lacking in a few others. Despite the general prominence of the shell, however, the characteristics that unify members of this group are mostly among their soft parts. The most readily recognized are a muscular foot, generally used for locomotion, and folds of skin, called a mantle, which may cover the upper part of the animal's body.

Most of the mollusks important to early Islanders are among the gastropods, which are characterized by a single shell. This feature distinguishes them from the clam and its relatives, which have paired shells. In old Hawaii, the gastropods, as a group, were recognized as varieties of *pūpū* (53). Nowadays this term commonly refers to an *hors d'oeuvre*, probably because various small gastropods

Plate 68. Orange cup coral, *Tubastrea coccinea.*

like ʻopihi (limpets) and *pipipi* (nerites) have long been popular snacks. The shells of the various gastropods are highly diverse, ranging in shape from the long slender augers to the cap-shaped limpets. And some, the nudibranchs, have no visible shell at all. This wide variation in form reflects diverse habits and habitats. Some mollusks thrive on rocky sea cliffs only now and then dampened by ocean spray, while others are suited to the sea floor at great depths offshore, and still others prefer one or another of the many habitats in between.

The most sought-after mollusks along rocky shores were, and still are, the limpets. Hawaiians have long recognized these as various kinds of ʻopihi and put them to widespread use not only as food, but also as medicine (53). And because the shells have sharp edges, they were used to scoop, scrape, or peel in a variety of tasks (53). Three kinds of ʻopihi were gathered: ʻopihi kōʻele *(Cellana talcosa)*, the largest, growing to about 4 inches long, but the most difficult to collect because it lives underwater or on sharp vertical faces of sea cliffs; ʻopihi ʻālinalina *(C. sandwicensis)*, the favorite even though it grows to only about 1.5 inches long and collecting was risky because it lives at the water's edge in places where the seas are particularly rough; and ʻopihi makaiaūli *(C. exarata)*, which also grows to about 1.5 inches long, lives higher on the rocks than the other two, and so was the most accessible (31, 53). Another gastropod with habits similar to the above, but only distantly related to them despite a similar shell, is *Siphonaria normalis.* Islanders called this species ʻopihi ʻawa, and although they rejected it as food because of a bitter taste, *kāhuna* put it to ceremonial use (53).

When taking ʻopihi from the rocks it was important to move quickly, because once touched they secure a firm grip and become very difficult to dislodge. Nowadays a knife is used to pry them loose, but in the old days the job was done with a sharp-edged stone. As a reminder of this early practice, the gathering of ʻopihi even today is referred to as kuʻi ʻopihi, or "ʻopihi pounding" (53). Although ʻopihi gatherers frequently popped these morsels into their mouths during their work, it was *kapu* for anyone ashore to do so while the gatherer was still out on the rocks. It was believed that if this *kapu* was broken, the gatherer would be washed away by the sea (53). Whether or not there was substance to this belief, certainly there were real dangers in ʻopihi gathering. The constant threat of being surprised and struck by an unusually large wave made it standard practice to face the sea whenever engaged in this activity (53), a practice that remains in effect today. Despite this precaution, however, many were lost, as evidenced by one old name for these animals, *he iʻa make,* or "creature of death" (53).

Even today careless *'opihi* gatherers occasionally are lost when swept from the rocks into the sea.

Rocky shores are also home for the nerites, which Hawaiians called *pipipi*, and for the littorines, which they called *'ākōlea*. Although these little gastropods are less than an inch long, Islanders have long collected them for food. In old Hawaii, however, pregnant women avoided eating the tiny black *pipipi* because it was believed that this would result in their child being born with small eyes (53). The *pipipi* are exposed on the rocks during both day and night and thus were available to the natives at all hours. Included among these is *Nerita picea*, the most common of the Hawaiian nerites. But a close relative, *Nerita polita*, which Islanders distinguished as *kūpe'e*, is exposed and thus available only at night (31).

The gastropods of rocky shores often are left high and dry by a receding tide, and at these times they clamp tightly on the rocks. But when they are submerged by a rising tide or bathed by breaking waves, they move slowly over the rocks, scraping off the fine algae that is their food. They do this using a tonguelike rasping structure called a radula. The radula, a unique feature of gastropods, takes different forms in different species, depending on its use.

Most gastropods live below the intertidal zone, and though less accessible then their relatives at the water's edge, many nevertheless were important to early Islanders. The two largest—the triton's trumpet, *Charonia tritonis* (Plate 69), and the helmet, *Cassis cornuta* (Plate 70) —were used not only for food, but also as trumpets or horns. By blowing into a small hole filed in the apex or pointed end of the shell, one can produce a low resonant sound. Today, as in times past, the sounds produced with helmet and triton shells introduce many Hawaiian ceremonies. As trumpets, the shells of both were known to Islanders as *pū*; otherwise the triton was distinguished as *pū puhi*, and the helmet as *pū ho'okani* (53). The triton, which grows to at least 18 inches long, lives among volcanic rocks and coral, where it feeds primarily at night on sea stars and sea urchins. In contrast, the helmet, which grows to about 12 inches long, lives in sand (31).

Members of several groups of gastropods remain inactive in rocky crevices or under boulders during the day and range into exposed locations when active at night. Included among these are the cowries, which were known to Islanders as various kinds of *leho*. Cowries are characterized by highly polished, colorful shells that make them especially attractive. Their glossy finish is maintained by secretions from the mantle, which completely covers the shell when the animal is active (Plate 71). Use of certain cowries as lures in capturing octopods is described below.

Another prominent gastropod active at night is the par-

Plate 69. Shell of the triton's trumpet, *Charonia tritonis*, occupied by the hermit crab *Aniculus maximus*.

Plate 70. Helmet, *Cassis cornuta.*

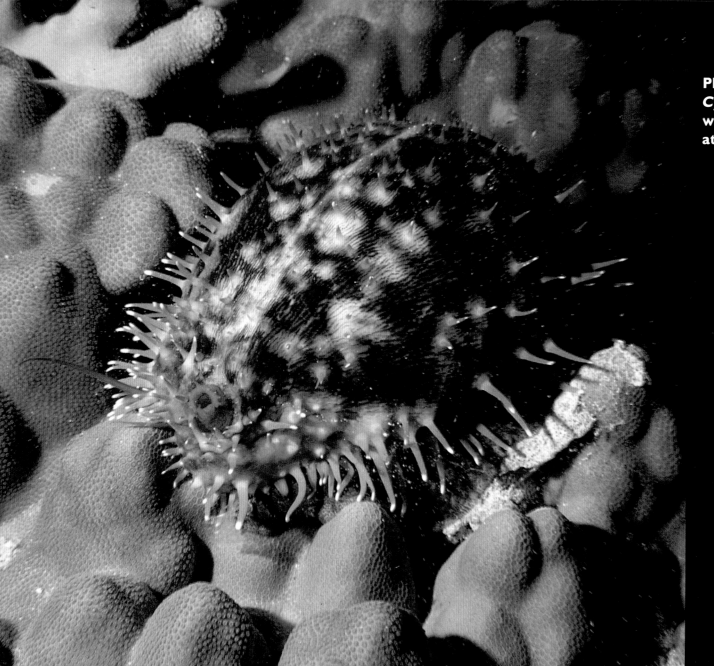

Plate 71. Tiger cowrie, *Cypraea tigris (leho)*, with mantle expanded at night.

tridge tun, *Tonna perdix* (Plate 72). After spending the day hidden in the sand, this animal emerges with darkness and hunts sea cucumbers and bivalved mollusks on the reef (31). Although the partridge tun attains a length of about 7 inches, one does not often see it alive. Its shell, however, is frequently found inhabited by the hermit crab *Aniculus maximus*. Once the shell has been occupied, the crab seeks out one or two anemones, *Calliactis armillatus*, which it places on the shell (51). Apparently these anemones, which have tentacles armed with stinging cells, protect the crab.

The cones, which live in many different habitats, present a variety of colorful shells. These animals are predators that subdue their prey with a potent venom injected into their victims through their radulas, which in these species have developed as long, hollow structures (31). The sting of some can painfully wound humans, and in fact one species common on Hawaiian reefs, *Conus textile*, has caused fatalities elsewhere in the Pacific (31). The cones that can sting humans were distinguished by Islanders as *pūpū pōniuniu*, or "dizzy shell"; the others were called *pūpū'alā* (53).

Although it is the shell that draws the attention of collectors to most mollusks, some of the most spectacularly beautiful animals in the sea belong to a group of gastropods that do not have visible shells at all. These are the nudibranchs, or sea slugs, a large assemblage that includes many different families. Most are very small animals, 1 inch long or less, but a few grow to a length of 1 foot or so. Usually they live on the sea floor, but some swimming forms undulate gracefully through the water. Nudibranchs must be seen in life to be appreciated, as they deteriorate quickly upon death, and the features that make them so attractive cannot be saved with preservatives.

The second largest group of mollusks are the bivalves, which differ from the gastropods in having two shells rather than one. Known generally as *'ōlepe* to Hawaiians, they include the clams and oysters. Although these are fewer and less diverse than the gastropods, some have long been highly valued by Islanders.

The pearl oysters were among the more sought-after bivalves in old Hawaii. The shells of these animals, called *uhi*, were highly valued as material for fish hooks, but the demand so exceeded the supply that in many regions their use had to be supplemented with other materials, including bone (53). Pearl oysters also were among the relatively few bivalves highly valued as food. The most common pearl oyster around the major islands, *Pinctada radiata*, was called *pipi*. Early Hawaiians gathered *pipi* in silence, because they believed that if they spoke the winds would blow and the *pipi* would drop from sight (53). Perhaps this belief developed from the likelihood

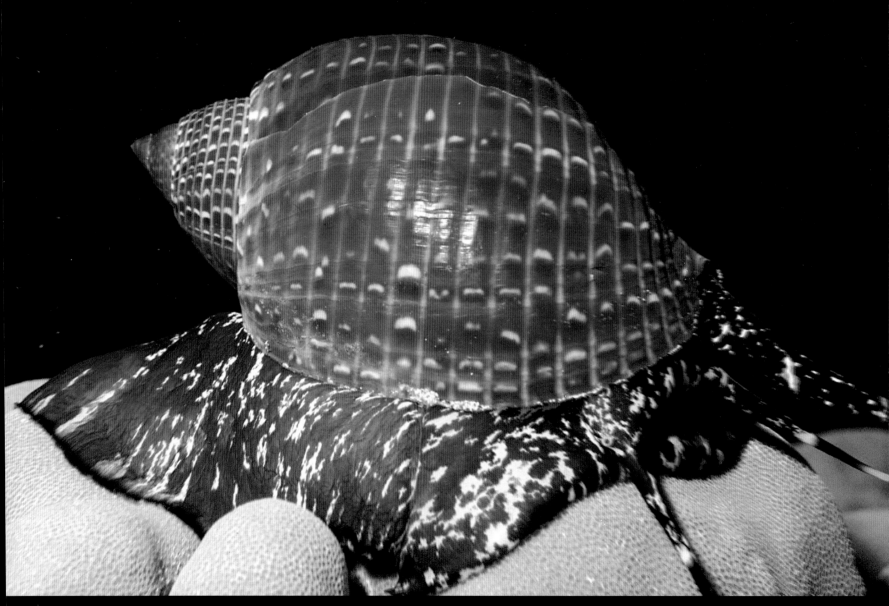

Plate 72. Partridge tun, *Tonna perdix.*

that conversation would involve unnecessary movement that might disturb the surface of the water. If not that, it might at least distract from the concerted effort needed during this activity to avoid disturbing the surface. *Pipi* were first located from above water, and a glassy surface was needed to effectively see through to the sea floor. Certainly any disturbance of this surface while fishing would have reduced visibility into the water and might well cause the oysters to "drop from sight."

Similarly, disturbance at the water's surface would have hampered fishing for another favored food, the rock oyster, *Chama iostoma*, which the natives called *kupekala*. These were obtained by diving to the sea floor and knocking them free with a rock (53). But before doing this, the natives first had to spot their quarry from above the water. And because these animals look much like the rocks to which they are attached, seeing them probably required the water to be clear and its surface to be glassy. To some extent fishermen could smooth the surface by chewing up and spitting upon the water a mouthful of *kukui* nuts (7). But not until the glass-bottom box was introduced in more recent times could they count on an underwater view free of distortions from surface disturbance.

The third major group among the mollusks are the cephalopods, which include the squids and octopods. These are curious creatures with a well-developed head that projects into a circle of eight or ten large, prehensile tentacles. Most do not have shells. Although only a few cephalopods are common in Hawaii, these were well known to early Islanders.

Two species of octopods, called *he'e*, occur on Island reefs: *Octopus ornatus* (Plate 73), which Islanders called *he'e pū loa*, and *O. cyanea*, which they called *he'e mauli* (31). Today fishermen commonly call both species "squid," even though animals more properly called squid have been recognized by Islanders as a different group of animals since ancient times. *O. ornatus* is known as the "night squid," based on its hunting in exposed places on the reef after dark, after spending the day resting out of sight (8). *O. cyanea*, on the other hand, is known as the "day squid," because it forages on the reef by day, mainly on crabs and shrimps (31). The cephalopods more properly called "squid" were known to early Hawaiians as *muhe'e*. Although these frequently occur over reefs, they are not reef creatures, but rather free-swimming inhabitants of the open ocean.

He'e and *mūhe'e* are still important as food in Hawaii, even though the flesh of both is tough and must be boiled or pounded before eating. Some early Islanders considered *he'e* and *mūhe'e* to be *'aumākua* (10) and used them as remedies for certain illnesses. The word *he'e* means to

111

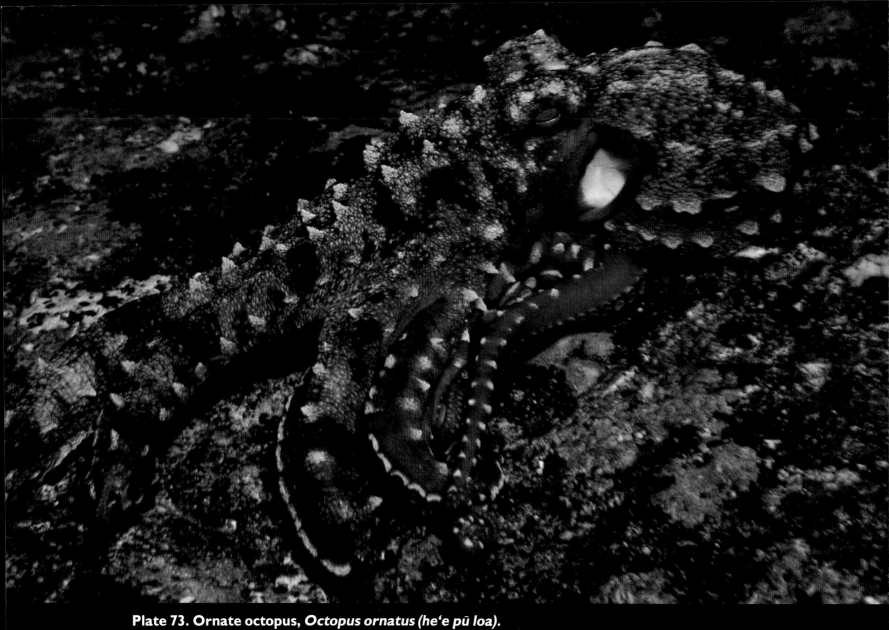

Plate 73. Ornate octopus, *Octopus ornatus* (he‘e pū loa).

dissolve, disperse, or put to flight, so probably preparations made from these animals were thought capable of driving away a malady (34). Several of the chants concerning these animals used in ancient times by *kāhuna* or fishermen are still heard today in Hawaiian songs and *hula.*

He'e have long been fished by a variety of methods. The simplest is to poke sticks into holes in the reef likely to harbor *he'e* and then spear or grasp the animal when it is driven into the open (7). In old Hawaii this was generally a task of women, many of whom became highly adept at spotting these animals in their hiding places (53). Another method used in the old days was to dangle one or more cowrie shells above a hole known to contain a *he'e.* Only those cowries that have spots against a reddish-brown ground were effective, however, which sharply limited the choice of shells that could be used. *He'e* have a particular attraction to cowries of this type and were captured when they left their holes to get them (7).

When *he'e* are in the open at night, fishermen take them by spear or by hand after spotting them under the light of a torch. An octopus in hand, however, is by no means an octopus captured. These writhing, muscular creatures, covered with mucus, are difficult to deal with —particularly when knee-deep in water at night with a torch in one hand. One can imagine the countless struggles that ensued on Island reef flats before fishermen resorted to one favored way of subduing a writhing *he'e,* that being to bite it between the eyes.

From early times the ink sac of the octopus (a structure that holds a dark fluid that is discharged when the animal is threatened) has been used as a basic ingredient in fish baits. There were many variations in its use, however, with each fisherman developing his own favorite recipe. All started with an ink sac, which Islanders called *'ala'ala he'e,* that had been roasted over coals in leaves of the *kiwi* plant and then ground to paste in a mortar. From here the individual fishermen were creative. Some added flowers of the *'ilima* plant—always some even number because odd numbers were believed to lack force. Others used *noni* leaves in the same way. The variations went on and on, but in the old days were limited to naturally occurring products. As other cultures entered the Islands during the nineteenth century, however, fishermen still searching for the perfect bait embellished their basic recipes with such ingredients as brandy and Perry Davis Pain Killer (7).

Shrimps, Lobsters, and Crabs

Animals that modern biologists call crustaceans include the familiar shrimps, crabs, and lobsters, as well as a variety of smaller creatures. A characteristic of crustaceans is

113

their encasement in a rigid, armorlike shell—an external skeleton. This affords the animal effective protection, but also creates problems in movement and growth. The armor is arranged in discrete sections, joined by articular membranes that permit movement between the different sections. Medieval knights might well have had crustacean anatomy in mind when designing their metallic armored suits, because they solved the problem of movement in the same way. Growth is attained by periodically shedding the outer shell, a process called molting, during which the animal ruptures its body shell and then pulls itself out. The new shell, already formed under the old one, is still soft and pliable, and once free of its discarded encasement the animal quickly increases in size before its new shell hardens. Once this has happened, no further growth is possible until the next molt.

Of the smaller crustaceans, the shrimps are prominent members of the reef community, and Islanders referred to them in general as ʻōpae (53). Fishing for ʻōpae usually was the task of women, who were highly proficient in the methods used. In going after ʻōpae on the reef, the fisherwomen held a cone-shaped basket in one hand and waded to depths where only their heads remained above water. There they forced their free hand into crevices and under rocks, thus driving the ʻōpae out into the basket, which was positioned to receive them (7). This was an effective way to catch ʻōpae, but a variety of species was taken and there was no practical reason to differentiate between them.

Apparently most of the reef shrimps now distinguished as species were not recognized as distinct by early Hawaiians, probably because no practical advantage was gained in doing so. Various types were defined based on distinctive features held in common, but generally this involved grouping numbers of species together. For example, the many species that have a beaklike projection, or rostrum, extending forward from their heads were known, collectively, as ʻōpae kākala, or "spiked shrimp" (53). Among the more common of them, *Saron marmoratus* (Plate 74) is distinguished today as the spiked prawn. Perhaps the most distinctive of the frequently observed shrimps on the reef, however, is *Stenopus hispidus* (Plate 75). Today this small species is distinguished as the banded coral shrimp, but early Islanders, ever pragmatic, apparently grouped it along with other shrimps that live in the sea as one of the ʻōpae kai. This designation distinguished them from the ʻōpae kuahiwi, or "mountain shrimp," which lived in the freshwater streams (53).

That shrimps living on the reef generally were distinguished by Islanders only as groups of species undoubtedly was due in part to their small size, as most are less than an inch or two long. It is significant that one freshwater

Plate 74. Spiked prawn, *Saron marmoratus* ('ōpae kākala).

Plate 75. Banded coral shrimp, *Stenopus hispidus* ('ōpae kai).

shrimp, *Macrobrachium grandimanus*, recognized by Islanders as a distinct form, *'ōpae 'oeha'a*, or "crooked-walking shrimp," is an exceptionally large, readily recognized species that was heavily fished in taro patches and streams (53).

The spiny lobsters, recognized as various forms of *ula*, are similar to shrimps, but grow much larger. The two major species, *Panulirus penicillatus* (Plate 76) and *P. marginatus*, commonly grow to about 18 inches long and attain weights of several pounds. The two are similar in appearance, and although they live at different depths in the northwestern Hawaiian Islands, they occur in similar habitats around the populated major islands (54). It remains uncertain whether early Islanders distinguished between them, although one old name, *ula hiwa*, or "black lobster" (39), may have referred to *P. marginatus*, which is much the darker of the two. At night both species are active in exposed locations, but during the day they retire to holes in the reef, often congregating in large numbers.

Ula have been much sought after by fishermen since ancient times. They have always been highly valued as food, and in the old days they also served as offerings in ceremonies that called for pigs when these were unavailable (53). In preparing them as food, the old practice of broiling them over coals remains popular today. But another old practice—eating them in a decomposed state, running out of the shell (53)—has few, if any, modern adherents.

Ula have long been hunted by divers who swam down to the reef and pulled them from their holes by hand. To do this, the hand must be protected, because although spiny lobsters do not have pincers, their bodies are heavily spined. In the old days divers protected their hands by wrapping them in cloth (7), but nowadays gloves are usually worn.

The slipper lobsters are closely related to the spiny lobsters, but look very different because of their flattened shape. The three species that live on Hawaiian reefs are distinctive, but it remains uncertain whether they were differentiated by early Islanders. The Hawaiian name generally associated with these animals, *ula pāpapa*, or "flat lobster," is used today in general reference to the group, but in early times may have referred to the largest and most sought after of the three, *Scyllarides squammosus*. This species grows to about 12 inches long and is a prized catch even today. Another name associated with the group, *ula pehu*, or "swollen lobster" (53), may have referred to *Parribacus antarcticus*, which has much the widest body. This species grows to about 8 inches long, but is little fished because its flattened body makes it difficult to see against the reef, and also because it carries

Plate 76. Spiny lobster,
Panulirus penicillatus
(ula).

relatively little meat. The third species, *Arctides regalis* (Plate 77), is the most colorful of the three, but with a maximum size of about 6 inches and a tendency to occur in deeper water (51), this species may well have escaped the attention of early Islanders. Like the spiny lobsters, the slipper lobsters are nocturnal. During the day, they are even more secretive than the *ula* and generally occur in exposed locations only after dark.

The reefs are home to a great variety of crabs, and many were important to Islanders. As a group they were called *pāpa'i*, and as was true with other groups of animals, species or groups of species were distinguished only when there was a practical reason to do so. The rock crab *Grapsus grapsus*, a species widely used as food, medicine, and a ceremonial sacrifice, was distinguished as *'a'ama* (53). This crab is common along rocky shores, where it scurries about at the water's edge. It was particularly sought after at times when rough seas prevented fishermen from seeking other species offshore (53). Unlike most crustaceans, which are nocturnal, *'a'ama* are active by day, and this made them even more available. They are agile, elusive creatures, however, and to catch them Islanders often used a line baited with *'opihi* (7), the shoreline gastropod described above. An alternate meaning of the word *'a'ama*, "to relax a grip," made ceremonial use relevant when the gods were being asked to relent and grant a request (53).

Most of the crabs that inhabit the subtidal reefs are members of the family Xanthidae. If one drags a large piece of coral rock out of the water and breaks it apart on the beach, an amazing number of tiny crabs scurry out from among the debris, and the vast majority of them are xanthids. Although most of the one hundred or so Island species in this family are small, one striking exception is the 7–11 crab, *Carpilius maculatus* (Plate 78), called *'alakuma*, which may be 6 inches across its shell (51). Legend attributes the prominent spots on this crab to a fight between one of its ancestors and a sea god. The crab's ancestor, suddenly seized by the god, struck back with its powerful pincers and drew blood from the attacker's fingers. The crab struggled free, but not before its shell was marked by bloody fingerprints. Again it was seized, and then again, but each time the result was the same. And today the 11 reddish-brown spots carried by the descendants of this crab remain as evidence of that ancient conflict (53).

Hermit crabs, called *pāpa'i iwi pūpū*, are adapted to life in abandoned gastropod shells. Whereas the abdomen of a typical crab is turned under the forward part of its body, that of the hermit crab projects backward as a soft, banana-shaped structure that fits into its adopted home. The front end of these crabs has the hard covering typical of other crustaceans, and when they withdraw into their shell many block the entrance with an enlarged pincer.

Plate 77. Regal slipper lobster, *Arctides regalis*.

Plate 78. 7–11 crab, *Carpilius maculatus* **('alakuma).**

As a hermit crab grows, it must periodically replace its adopted shell with a larger one. When a prospective replacement is found, the crab carefully examines the shell with its claws. If the shell is satisfactory, the crab quickly transfers its vulnerable abdomen to the new home. Sometimes one crab will attempt to pull another from a particularly desirable shell.

Many hermit crabs inhabit shallow water, the most common of these being species of the genus *Calcinus.* These crabs often congregate under boulders, and when these boulders are overturned the crabs scurry in all directions. The largest of Hawaiian hermit crabs, *Aniculus maximus*, usually occupies the shell of the triton (Plate 69).

Sea Urchins, Sea Stars, and Sea Cucumbers

Some of the most conspicuous animals on Hawaiian reefs are members of the group known to biologists as echinoderms, a word that means "spiny skin." Included here are the sea urchins, sea stars (starfishes), and sea cucumbers. Most members of this assemblage are encased in a skeleton of armorlike plates, on which are mounted spines or other projections. But the most striking characteristic shared by members of this group is a symmetrical posi-

tioning of body parts around a central point like spokes in a wheel. This gives them a top and a bottom, but in most cases not a front or back. In many species, however, these features can be recognized only with careful study, because each of the very different groups among the echinoderms has acquired distinctive variations on this generalized theme.

The sea urchins, or echinoids, are enclosed in globular skeletons, or tests, and most are heavily spined. The tests are hard and contain many small holes through which protrude small, flexible appendages called tube feet that, along with their movable spines, give these animals mobility. Most sea urchins are herbivores that use a beaklike feeding apparatus with five teeth to scrape fine algae off the surfaces of rocks and corals.

Three long-spined urchins, which Hawaiians recognized as varieties of *wana*, are hazardous to humans, but also have long been the most sought after as food. These are *Diadema paucispinum*, *Echinothrix calamaris* (Plate 79), and *E. diadema*. The primary threat from these animals comes not from their large, primary spines, however, but rather from their smaller, secondary spines, because it is these that are barbed and carry venom. Nevertheless, all the spines are brittle, and after puncturing the skin of an unfortunate fish or human they often break off deep within the wound. So in addition to the immedi-

Plate 79. Sea urchin, *Echinothrix calamaris* (wana).

ate intense pain caused by the venom, the victim may suffer a secondary infection as well. This threat of injury has not discouraged the collection of these urchins as food, but certainly it has introduced a strong element of caution into the operation.

The taking of these animals is seasonal, because it is their fully developed eggs that are eaten. This is evidenced in the old saying, "*pala ka hala, momona ka hā'uke'uke*, which means, "when the *hala* flowers are ripe, the sea eggs are fat" (53). *Wana* can be handled with care from the underside, where the spines are short, but before proceeding with preparations for eating all the spines must be removed. In the old days, usually this was done by striking them against a rock (53), but now it is common practice to place many of them together in a wire cage and shake until all the spines have broken off.

Although *wana* have received the most attention, the most numerous sea urchin in the Islands is the short-spined *Echinometra mathaei* (Plate 80). There are color variations of this species that early Islanders recognized as varieties of *'ina:* the reddish form was called *'ina 'ula*, the whitish-green form *'ina kea*, and the black form *'ina uli* (53). Probably because they are relatively small, *'ina* were not taken as food, except for preparation of a sauce, called *kai 'ina*, which was used with raw fish (53). The species is nevertheless an important force in eroding reefs (25). By continuously abrading a single spot on the reef,

each *'ina* gradually hollows out a pocket that shelters not only itself, but over time many other organisms that occupy the pocket after the urchin is gone. In this way, countless generations of *'ina* have produced extensively pitted surfaces on many reefs throughout the Islands.

The slate-pencil urchin, *Heterocentrotus mammillatus* (Plate 81), called *pūnohu* by early Islanders, has club-shaped spines that actually were used as "pencils" in the old days (53), but only as wind chimes and decorations in more recent times. Over the years, casual visitors to the reef, their attention drawn by this animal's unique characteristics, have thoughtlessly carried them ashore only to later discard them on the beach. The result of this unfortunate popularity is that in areas readily accessible to humans this creature is scarce.

A distinctive inhabitant of rocky shores, *Colobocentrotus atrata* (Plate 82), called *hā'uke'uke*, is highly specialized to a life clinging against rocks awash in the surf. The spines over the top of its flattened test are short and table-shaped, thus minimizing resistance to the rush of water, while the longer spines around the margin of its test, along with its tube feet, secure its grasp on the rocks. So tenacious is their hold that fishermen seeking them for food usually pry them loose with a knife in much the same way they collect *'opihi*. In ancient times the teeth of this urchin were valued as medicine (6).

The sea stars, or asteroids, are among the animals most

Plate 80. Sea urchin, _Echinometra mathaei_ ('ina uli).

Plate 81. Slate-pencil sea urchin, *Heterocentrotus mammillatus* (pūnohu).

Plate 82. Sea urchin, *Colobocentrotus atrata* (hāʻukeʻuke).

often perceived in the popular mind as creatures of the sea. The familiar arms of sea stars are not appendages, as one might suppose, but are in fact extensions of the body; each carries a segment of the reproductive organs, digestive tract, and other body components. This fact makes it easier to understand the remarkable ability of sea stars to regenerate parts of their bodies that have been lost. This ability is particularly well developed in the several species of *Linckia* on Hawaiian reefs. These can be recognized by their smooth, leatherlike skin and small central body with long, thin arms. Even a piece of the arm, when torn from one of these creatures, can reorganize itself into a whole new animal. Thus, if one is fragmented, a number of new animals will result.

Although several species of sea stars are common residents of the reef, none have Hawaiian names so far as is known. Probably this is because none are suitable for human food. In old Hawaii, one general name for the group was *pe'a*. A term sometimes seen today, *i'a hōkū*, is a modern translation of "star fish" (53).

A sea star that has attracted considerable notoriety in recent years is the crown-of-thorns, *Acanthaster planci* (Plate 83). This species has venomous spines, but the reason for its notoriety comes from its habit of eating corals. During recent decades this animal has appeared in exceptionally large numbers at various places in the Pacific Ocean, where it has done great damage to the reefs. Despite much concern about the long-lasting effects of this damage, however, there has been no indication that the crown-of-thorns is an unusual threat to Hawaiian reefs.

The sea cucumbers, or holothurians, are elongated, often sausage-shaped creatures that lie with little movement on the sea floor. When their body plan, as an echinoderm, is compared with that of the sea urchins or sea stars, sea cucumbers can be thought of as lying on their side. The sea urchin and sea star both have their mouth on their underside, facing the substrate, and their anus is directly opposite, on the top of their body. In contrast, the mouth and anus of sea cucumbers are located at either end of their long drawn-out body. Typically one side consistently lies against the substrate, so that their external body features have secondarily varied from the radial symmetry of the generalized echinoderm to a superficial bilateral symmetry. Usually on the side of the body that rests on the sea floor the tube feet are well developed, whereas on surfaces not in contact with the substrate these structures are reduced to wartlike protuberances or are lost completely. The sea cucumbers further differ from other echinoderms in that their skeleton is reduced to minute plates embedded in their integument, and as a feeding mechanism they have a circle of

Plate 83. Crown-of-thorns, *Acanthaster planci.*

tentacles around their mouth. These tentacles in many species shovel a continuous load of sand or mud into the mouth, and as this material moves through the gut the animal digests from it a great assortment of nutritive matter.

Sea cucumbers, called *loli* by Hawaiians, include the common *Holothuria atra* (Plate 84). The black leathery integument of this species usually is covered by a fine layer of sand. Like many other sea cucumbers, members of this species disgorge their internal organs when disturbed. They emit this material as a tangled, sticky mass, probably as a defense against predators. This loss of organs does not trouble them, however, because they soon regenerate another set. In some parts of the Pacific, natives deliber-ately agitate large sea cucumbers and then collect the disgorged organs for food. The bodies, too, of many sea cucumbers are highly regarded as food, usually after being boiled and then dried or smoked. In the early years of this century, all species of *loli* were an important food in Hawaii (7), but today *Stichopus horrens* is favored.

Sea cucumbers of the family Synaptidae are especially elongated and have body walls that are very thin and flexible. These snakelike creatures feed mostly on decaying matter that clings to seaweeds. One species, *Euapta godeffroyi* (Plate 85), is a denizen of exposed rocky coasts, where it is seen mostly at night. Another, *Opheodesoma spectabilis*, is a pinkish form occurring mostly in protected areas, like Kāneʻohe Bay on Oʻahu.

Plate 84. Sea cucumber, *Holothuria atra (loli)*.

Plate 85. Sea cucumber
Euapta godeffroyi.

References

1. Balazs, G. H. 1980. Synopsis of biological data on the green turtle in the Hawaiian Islands. NOAA Technical Memorandum, NMFS, NOAA-TM-NMFS-SWFC-7. 141 p.

2. Bardach, J. E. 1961. Transport of calcareous fragments by reef fishes. Science 133(3446): 98–99.

3. Barnes, R. D. 1980. Invertebrate zoology, 4th ed. Philadelphia: Saunders College. 1089 p.

4. Beckley, E. M. 1887. Hawaiian fisheries and methods of fishing with an account of the fishing implements used by natives of the Hawaiian Islands. U. S. Fish Commission, Bulletin 6:245–256.

5. Beckwith, M. W. 1917. Hawaiian shark aumakua. American Anthropologist 19:503–517.

6. Beckwith, M. W. 1932. Kepelino's traditions of Hawaii. Bernice P. Bishop Museum, Bulletin 95. 206 p.

7. Cobb, J. N. 1902. The commercial fisheries of the Hawaiian Islands. U. S. Commission of Fish and Fisheries, Commissioner's Report for 1900–1901: 383–499.

8. Edmondson, C. H. 1946. Reef and shore fauna of Hawaii. Bernice P. Bishop Museum, Special Publication 22. 381 p.

9. Eibl-Eibesfeldt, I. 1965. Land of a thousand atolls. London: MacGibbon and Key. 194 p.

10. Emerson, J. S. 1892. The lesser Hawaiian gods. Hawaiian Historical Society, paper 2. 24 p.

11. Emerson, N. B. 1909. Unwritten literature of Hawaii. Bureau of American Ethnology, Bulletin 38. Smithsonian Institution. 288 p.

12. Fornander, A. 1918–1919. Fornander collection of Hawaiian antiquities and folklore. Bernice P. Bishop Museum, Memoirs, vol. 5. 721 p.

13. Gosline, W. A. 1965. Thoughts on systematic work in outlying areas. Systematic Zoology 14:59–61.

14. Gosline, W. A., and V. E. Brock. 1960. Handbook of Hawaiian fishes. Honolulu: University of Hawaii Press. 372 p.

15. Halstead, B. 1959. Dangerous marine animals. Baltimore: Cornell Maritime Press. 146 p.

16. Helfrich, P., and A. H. Banner. 1960. Hallucinatory mullet poisoning. Journal of Tropical Medicine and Hygiene 63: 86–89.

17. Henderson, J. R. 1985. A review of Hawaiian monk seal entanglements in marine debris. NOAA Technical Memorandum, NMFS, NOAA-TM-NMFS-SWFC-54: 326–335.

18. Henderson, J. R. Honolulu Laboratory, National Marine Fisheries Service. Personal communication, 11 September 1989.

19. Hobson, E. S. 1963. Notes on piloting behavior in young yellow jacks. Underwater Naturalist 1(4): 10–13.

20. Hobson, E. S. 1968. Predatory behavior of some shore fishes in the Gulf of California. U. S. Fish and Wildlife Service, Research Report 73. 92 p.

21. Hobson, E. S. 1969. Possible advantages to the blenny *Runula azalea* in aggregating with the wrasse *Thalassoma lucasanum* in the tropical eastern Pacific. Copeia 1969 (1): 191–193.

22. Hobson, E. S. 1974. Feeding relationships of teleostean fishes on coral reefs in Kona, Hawaii. Fishery Bulletin 72:915–1031.

23. Hobson, E. S. 1979. Interactions between piscivorous fishes and their prey. *In* Predator-prey systems in fisheries management, ed. H. Clepper, pp. 231–242. Washington, D.C.: Sport Fishing Institute.

24. Hobson, E. S. 1984. The structure of reef fish communities in the Hawaiian archipelago. Proceedings of the second symposium on resource investigations in the northwestern Hawaiian Islands, vol. 1. Sea Grant Miscellaneous Report UNIHI-SEAGRANT-MR-84-01: 101–122.

25. Hodgkin, E. P. 1960. Patterns of life on rocky shores. Journal of the Royal Society of Western Australia 43:35–43.

26. Johanos, T. C., and S. L. Austin. 1983. Hawaiian monk seal population structure, reproduction and survival on Laysan Island, 1985. NOAA Technical Memorandum, NMFS, NOAA-TM-NMFS-118. 38 p.

27. Johnson, P. A., and B. W. Johnson. 1984. Hawaiian monk seal observations on French Frigate Shoals, 1980. NOAA Technical Memorandum, NMFS, NOAA-TM-NMFS-SWFC-50. 47 p.

28. Jones, R. S. 1968. Ecological relationships in Hawaiian and Johnston Island Acanthuridae (surgeonfishes). Micronesica 4:309–361.

29. Kalakaua, D. 1888. The legends and myths of Hawaii. New York: C. L. Webster Co. 530 p.

30. Kamakau, S. M. 1870. Story of Hawaii. *Ke Au Okoa*. 6 January 1870.

31. Kay, E. A. 1979. Hawaiian marine shells. Bernice P. Bishop Museum, Special Publication 64(4). 653 p.

32. Kenyon, K. W., and D. W. Rice. 1959. Life history of the Hawaiian monk seal. Pacific Science 13:215–252.

33. Losey, G. S., Jr. 1971. Communication between fishes in cleaning symbiosis. *In* Aspects of the biology of symbiosis, ed. T. Cheng, pp. 45–76. Baltimore: University Park Press.

34. Malo, D. 1903. Hawaiian antiquities. Bernice P. Bishop Museum, Special Publication 2. 366 p.

35. Manu, M. 1901. Ku'ula, the fish god of Hawaii. Translated by M. K. Nakuina. Hawaiian Almanac and Annual for 1901: 114–124.

36. Maragos, J. E. 1977. Order Scleractinia. *In* Reef and shore fauna of Hawaii, sec. 1: Protozoa through Ctenophora, eds. D. M. Devaney and L. G. Eldridge, pp. 158–241. Honolulu: Bishop Museum Press.

37. McAllister, J. G. 1933. Archaeology of Oahu. Bernice P. Bishop Museum, Bulletin 104. 201 p.

38. Motta, P. J. 1988. Functional morphology of the feeding apparatus of ten species of Pacific butterflyfishes (Perciformes, Chaetodontidae): An ecomorphological approach. Enviromental Biology of Fishes 22:39–67.

39. Pukui, M. K., and S. H. Elbert. 1986. Hawaiian dictionary. Honolulu: University of Hawaii Press. 572 p.

40. Randall, J. E. 1985. Guide to Hawaiian fishes. Newtown Square, Pa.: Harrowood Books. 79 p.

41. Reese, E. S. 1975. A comparative field study of the social behavior and related ecology of reef fishes of the famiy Chaetodontidae. Zeitschrift für Tierpsychologie 37:37–61.

42. Reinboth, R. 1962. Morphologische und funktionelle Zweigeschlechtlichkeit bei marinen Teleostiern (Serranidae, Sparidae, Centracanthidae, Labridae). Zoologische Jahrbücher Abteilung für Allgemeine Zoologie und Physiologie der Tiere 69:405–480.

43. Reinboth, R. 1968. Protogynie bei Papageifischen (Scaridae). Zeitschrift für Naturforschung 23b(6): 852–855.

44. Rice, W. H. 1923. Hawaiian legends. Bernice P. Bishop Museum, Bulletin 3. 137 p.

45. Richards, D. K. 1941. Men beat the sea and its gods. Honolulu Star-Bulletin, 1 March 1941.

46. Scheffer, V. B. 1958. Seals, sea lions and walruses. Stanford, Calif.: Stanford University Press. 179 p.

47. Schlexer, F. V. 1984. Diving patterns of the Hawaiian monk seal, Lisianski Island. NOAA Technical Memorandum, NMFS, NOAA-TM-NMFS-SWFC-41.

48. Stepien, C. A., and R. C. Brusca. 1985. Nocturnal attacks on nearshore fishes in southern California by crustacean zooplankton. Marine Ecology Progress Series 25:91–105.

49. Stone, H. S. 1984. Hawaiian monk seal population research, Lisianski Island, 1982. NOAA Technical Memorandum, NMFS, NOAA-TM-NMFS-SWFC-47. 33 p.

50. Strasburg, D. S. 1960. The blennies. In W. A. Gosline and V. E. Brock, Handbook of Hawaiian fishes, p. 277. Honolulu: University of Hawaii Press.

51. Tinker, S. W. 1965. Pacific Crustacea. Rutland, Vt.: Charles Tuttle. 134 p.

52. Titcomb, M., with M. K. Pukui, collaborator. 1972. Native use of fish in Hawaii. Honolulu: University of Hawaii Press. 175 p.

53. Titcomb, M., with D. B. Fellows, M. K. Pukui, and D. M. Devaney, collaborators. 1978. Native use of marine invertebrates in old Hawaii. Pacific Science 32:325–386.

54. Uchida, R. N., and D. T. Tagami. 1984. Biology, distribution, population structure and pre-exploitation abundance of spiny lobster, *Panulirus marginatus*, in the northwestern Hawaiian Islands. Proceedings of the second symposium on resource investigations in the northwestern Hawaiian Islands, vol. 1. Sea Grant Miscellaneous Report UNIHI-SEAGRANT-MR-84-01: 157–198.

55. Uchiyama, J. T., and D. T. Tagami. 1984. Life history, distribution and abundance of bottomfishes in the northwestern Hawaiian Islands. Proceedings of the second symposium on resource investigations in the northwestern Hawaiian Islands, vol. 1. Sea Grant Miscellaneous Report UNIHI-SEAGRANT-MR-84-01: 229–247.

56. Winn, H. E., and J. E. Bardach. 1959. Differential food selection by moray eels and a possible role of the mucous envelope of parrotfishes in reduction of predation. Ecology 40(2): 296–298.

About the Authors

Edmund Hobson is a research biologist with the National Oceanographic and Atmospheric Administration (NOAA). He received his B.A. and M.S. degrees from the University of Hawaii and his Ph.D. from the University of California at Los Angeles. He has studied and photographed Hawaiian reef animals for more than thirty years (all the photographs in this book are by him). Based on these and other studies done elsewhere he has published fifty-four articles on behavior and ecology of reef animals.

E. H. Chave is a researcher at the University of Hawaii Undersea Research Laboratory, where she is responsible for the data obtained by the laboratory's two submersibles. She has received degrees from the University of California at Berkeley, Stanford University, and the University of Hawaii, and has published numerous articles on various marine creatures. Her next book is about large Hawaiian marine animals found at bottom depths of from 50 to 2000 meters.

Production Notes

This book was designed by Roger Eggers.
Composition and paging were done on the
Quadex Composing System and typesetting
on the Compugraphic 8400 by the design
and production staff of University of
Hawaii Press.

The text typeface is Trump and the
display typeface is Gill Sans Medium.

Offset presswork and binding were done by
Golden Cup Printing Co., Ltd. in Hong Kong.